TRUCKING BUSINESS STARTUP

THE COMPLETE STEP-BY-STEP GUIDE TO STARTING & MAINTAINING A SUCCESSFUL TRUCKING COMPANY EVEN IF YOU'RE AN ABSOLUTE BEGINNER

WALTER GRANT

GARY FIELD

CONTENTS

INTRODUCTION

Dream big; Start small;

But most of all...Start!

-by Simon Sinek

Recent statistics show that logistics and warehousing are in more demand than ever. Modern consumers prefer online shopping for all their daily needs, making these industries extremely competitive. Trucks are a crucial part of this supply chain. Trucks in the United States transport over 70% of the freight goods nationwide. Financial experts predict that this industry will experience a 27% growth in the next decade, making it an ideal investment. Furthermore, over 90% of the companies in the trucking industry have less than six trucks, meaning that the small carriers currently dominate industry.

Many people want to invest in this incredible industry, but they are hesitant to take the first step. The task of securing capital to begin this journey is daunting, but it is doable. Starting a trucking company is not only meant for big corporations! Ordinary people can start and maintain a successful trucking business in as little as four weeks. If you have the determination, creativity, and proper guidance, you can make it happen.

This book is a guide designed to help the following people.

- **Truck drivers who have been working for a long time**: These professionals work for many hours just to make ends meet. They already have the right expertise to start their business and enjoy the freedom of being their own boss.
- **People who are passionate about the trucking business:** These people may or may not have any experience in running a trucking business. These individuals, however, are willing to learn the basics of the industry from scratch.
- **Individuals who want to increase their income:** The cost of living has gone up significantly in recent years. Having just one income is not enough for a family. If you want to increase your income, the trucking business is an excellent side hustle.
- **People who need a home-based investment:** Running successful businesses is always challenging

because of the costs involved. Operational costs can hinder many people in their business goals. You can comfortably run a trucking business in the comfort of your home, reducing numerous costs.

In this book, you will learn how to write your business plan and raise the necessary capital to run your company. You will learn basic legal and licensing requirements for your operation. We will point you in the direction of the right professionals—those you need to help run your business successfully. We will discuss marketing, pricing, and collection strategies that work! You will learn the best ways to source your trucks, and you will see how to incorporate technology into your business. In the end, you will be able to avoid the most common pitfalls and start your modern trucking business.

The authors of this book are renowned business experts. These professionals understand the business world. Their goal is to help newbies get into the trucking business. Walter Grant is a talented and creative businessman who has spent most of his career in the business world. Gary Field, on the other hand, specializes in the freight and transport sectors of the industry. With his expansive skills in this profitable market, Field will equip you with the skills you need to kick-start your business.

Starting a business scares away many people in the world today because of the challenges involved. When you have guidance from seasoned entrepreneurs, however, the journey is much easier.

After reading this book, you will understand everything about starting a trucking business, making good profits, and becoming your own boss.

CHAPTER 1
STEP ONE: ARE YOU UP TO THE CHALLENGE?

N ow more than ever, the trucking industry is the backbone of the American economy. If the small businesses in this sector decided to close shop, the United States economy would come to a screeching halt. The current driver shortages paired with the increased freight demand simply mean that you have a great chance to make profits and enjoy financial freedom for a long time to come (Digital Edge, 2021).

Being the owner of a trucking company is not always a walk in the park; your role is integral to the daily operations. After building my business, I have realized that this industry is challenging and fast paced.

RESPONSIBILITIES

First, before I explain my daily activities, I want to point out the responsibilities of a trucking business owner. As the owner of this new business, you are considered responsible for

- the overall performance of your fleet
- the ability to meet delivery deadlines as promised
- the management of your business to produce profits
- the training, supervision, and development of employees
- the schedule on which your entire company operates

A TYPICAL DAY

Every day will be different when running your trucking business. The following, however, are the mandatory things to do on a normal working day.

1. **Administrative:** It is your job to ensure that drivers are compensated for their time and efforts. You must also ensure that all compliances in the company remain up to date.
2. **Relationship Management**: Most of your time should be spent creating and maintaining good relationships with your drivers. The current driver shortage makes it critical to retain your hardworking

drivers. Communication and trust between owner and drivers lead to solid professional relationships and loyalty.

3. **Operational**: You must always know when your trucks are due for maintenance; trucks in good condition deliver results on time. It is up to you to create and maintain the schedule. You should know where your drivers are at all times. Clear communication with your drivers means that you will avoid late deliveries and other problems on the road.

PERSONAL CHARACTERISTICS AND SKILLS

Every business in the world comes with its share of challenges. Certain traits and skills are necessary to navigate common issues and build a profitable business.

- **Ability to multitask**: Being the leader of a business will force you to become comfortable multitasking all the time. You will need to balance and prioritize daily activities and timelines (Transport Topics, 2017). Failure will result in numerous delays.
- **Patience**: You need to expect some delays and be able to tolerate uncertainty in the business. In the transport industry, unexpected things happen—daily. When you face a tough situation, be patient while searching for an ideal solution.

- **Excellent communication skills:** Your drivers will receive instructions from you every single day. On a typical day, you will speak to clients, dispatchers, and shop managers. Without the right communication skills, your company will be ruined. This includes listening to what your drivers are telling you. Together you will find solutions when problems arise.
- **Organized:** Managers must be organized for the sake of their business. Disorganized transport is a recipe for wasted time and lost deadlines.
- **Problem solver:** Your company needs a creative person. Always seek effective solutions to any problems facing your company.
- **Confidence** – Whenever you must make decisions for your trucking business, it is paramount to be confident. Remember, you are the leader of the fleet.

WHY CHOOSE THE TRUCKING INDUSTRY?

Venturing into the world of trucking will give you the opportunity to enjoy several industry-wide benefits.

Flexible Schedules

When working as a trucker, you have the freedom to set your own schedule. Drivers can choose the workload they need and have enough work-life balance to enjoy the money they make. When you first start your business, you might need to spend more time and resources on building your clientele and reputation. With time, however, you will earn repeat customers, and this means you can hire other drivers to help carry the load. When you divide your total workload amongst your multiple drivers, it allows flexibility in your schedule. Do not be intimidated about the workload in the beginning! Many people have done this before, and they have achieved great success (K & J Trucking, 2018).

No College Degree Required

Your college degree should never determine your destiny. You can have a successful career without a college degree. Trucking is one of the industries that does not require many years of expensive higher education. If the idea of learning a trade inspires you more than the thought of four years in university, the trucking business is a great place to explore. It all begins with your drivers' license. Then, you will need to complete your Commercial Driving License (CDL) training. When you have the legal requirements, you can hit the open roads to make your living.

Earn Good Money

At the end of the day, it is profit that will attract investors to a business. Nobody wants to sink time and money into a fruitless, risky venture. With the current market and consumer habits, your trucking company will stay in high demand. The biggest determining factor of how much yearly income you make will be how much work you put into it. Once you set up the business properly, your work ethic will net you the income you are looking for.

Become a Professional Tourist

Being a truck driver, you will have the opportunity to travel to various parts of the country and get paid while doing it. Many drivers look forward to the long trips because they enjoy visiting unfamiliar places. Drivers travel through all fifty states, and every drive is a new exciting experience (Faster Truck, n.d).

High Demand

The trucking industry has undergone numerous changes in the past two years. The pandemic has established the need for professionals in this sector. More and more, customers prefer online shopping to busy and crowded stores. Warehousing and logistics have been forced to grow and adjust significantly because of the demand for fast shipping. Truck transportation is a crucial link in the supply chain for any business trying to get their products into the hands of consumers. Without trucks, moving goods from one place to another becomes cost-prohibitive and exponentially more difficult.

Analysts' reports indicate that the American trucking industry is strong and will continue to experience the current demands into 2022 and beyond. Even as government leaders, health agencies, and local businesses begin to relax restrictions, demand for truck transportation will continue to grow. Once people feel more comfortable, consumer spending is expected to increase. This means that not only will customers expect fast shipping times for online orders, but stores will need more inventory and supplies to sell.

THE FUTURE LOOKS BRIGHT

Wise business professionals must consider the future of their investments. It is not easy to predict the future of any business. However, investors make decisions after observing past behaviors. The past few months have been tough for many businesses in the world. The United States economy, however, could improve in the coming months (Transport Topics 2021) Every industry has its share of challenges. The transportation sector is no different. Small companies in this industry are dealing with some big problems. The biggest problem at the moment is recruiting enough qualified truck drivers. Due to the increased demand for trucking services, companies are in search of drivers now more than ever. If you have been dreaming about starting a trucking business, this is the best time to do it.

CHAPTER 2
STEP TWO: DIFFERENT TYPES OF TRUCKING COMPANIES

Perhaps before you go any further, it is important to know that there are several types of companies within the trucking business. Not all companies specialize in the same services. Many drivers tend to overlook this, and they may end up with unrealized expectations. The difference in the type of transport company, according to experts, plays a significant role in the income and overall experience of the drivers. By understanding each subsector, you can pick one that best suits your career path.

FOR-HIRE TRUCKLOAD CARRIERS

The for-hire truckload carriers earn money by hauling freight from other organizations. When you decide to work for a for-hire truckload carrier, you will be working for an organization that does not produce or manufacture consumer goods. These companies make their money by contracting out their fleet capacity to manufacturing companies who need to transport their goods from one place to the other. Since hired truckload carriers never manufacture any products, their workload depends on the demands of other organizations.

While there are benefits to this, there are a few disadvantages to establishing this type of company (Everton, 2017). For-hire businesses must bid to get work from companies that manufacture goods. It takes research, work, and determination to win bids for great companies, and, technically, a contract is only guaranteed work for a specified time. You will constantly have to compete with other companies who will continue to bid for the freight contract. As the owner of a hired fleet, you must always be aware of the changes in the freight market because a single mistake could cost you a contract.

PRIVATE FLEETS

Many companies in the market manufacture their products and take charge of their distribution chain. A private fleet is only part of a company who manufactures their goods and supply those commodities using trucks, drivers, and trailers. A truck driver who chooses to work for a private fleet is an employee of the freight company.

For example, Red Bird is a private fleet. Red Bird produces a certain product. They have their own drivers who deliver their manufactured products to various parts of the country. These companies rarely need help from other companies when it comes to their freight. When the need arises, however, Red Bird can employ the use of a for-hire company to transport their goods.

Working for a private fleet comes with several benefits. Monthly take-home pay is typically higher for fleet drivers, and they are some of the most experienced professionals in the business.

The greatest disadvantage of working for these companies is that your employer will always determine your job security. If your employer goes bankrupt, you will be looking for a new job. Drivers' wages may suffer if the company's products fall out of favor with consumers. Simply put, drivers working for private fleets put all their eggs in one basket.

LESS-THAN-TRUCKLOAD CARRIERS

When an item is too big for the postal services, these well-known carriers step in. Several trucking companies in the American market operate less-than-truckload freight. Popularly known as LTL, these companies help thousands of customers ship and receive goods to and from destinations all over the country.

The LTL companies in America operate 53 foot long trailers that move small products to various distribution centers, and then smaller delivery trucks transport the goods to residential or commercial locations. One LTL delivery truck is capable of transporting over 30 different goods for different customers across the country. LTL companies employ their own drivers —for both the larger tractor trailers and the smaller delivery trucks.

When you start an LTL Company, you will need to employ two kinds of drivers. The first driver is typically required to transport the freight from a hub to a sorting facility by way of a tractor trailer or large transport truck. These drivers typically have designated schedules and consistent miles. This makes it easier for them to have some regular home time.

The second operates like a typical city driver. This driver will run their designated route in a delivery truck, making local stops for pick-ups or deliveries along the way. These workers go home every single day, but they deal with daily issues like traffic and heavy workloads. They also act as the LTL's public facing employees and will need to be able to deal appropriately with customers.

HOUSEHOLD MOVERS

Household movers are a special type of trucking company. They help their customers to move from one residence to another and settle down. Responsibilities in household moving companies are very different from all the other types of trucking businesses because movers offer more than just transport services.

Movers can offer various relocation packages to their customers. Drivers might also help to pack the goods, load, and offload boxes and items for the customers. Not everyone enjoys the physical labor required in these situations. Positions in these businesses are suitable for professionals who love physical labor.

The biggest disadvantage of working for these companies is the increased risk of injury. There is a lot of physical labor that might cause severe damage to vital parts of the human body if proper precautions are not taken. Aside from injury, there is a risk that a mover might end up in a less than desirable environment. It is not always possible for the business owner or driver to know the state of the household items they will be transporting or the condition of the houses they will be entering (Everton, 2017).

INTER-MODAL

Trucks are not the only method of moving consumer goods from the manufacturer to other parts of the country. Some manufacturing companies also use methods such as railway transport to move their freight across the country. This process can be more expensive and more complicated than the previously mentioned types of businesses.

In inter-modal companies, the distribution process is multi-layered, and you will need more people to complete a delivery. Your company would assist clients by delivering goods to the rail yard first. Then, once the freight has been transported by rail closer to the final destination, your company would then pick up the freight and deliver it to the customer.

The best thing about inter-modal companies is that they need more drivers to get their products into the customers' hands. This means more job opportunities. You can start an inter-model company if you live near a rail hub or a major shipping port. Making your company available in places like this will typically net you very lucrative contracts with those companies who use railway transportation in addition to trucks.

Regardless of the company you choose to start in your trucking journey, the returns will always be excellent. The most important thing to do is to learn everything about the type of organization you need.

CHAPTER 3
STEP THREE: CREATE YOUR BUSINESS PLAN

S tarting a business is tough, regardless of the industry you select. With the right preparations, however, it is possible for new businesses to become successful in a competitive market. Having a business plan that outlines your goals is one of the most important things for your new business. When you need funds from financial institutions and business partners, a business plan will be mandatory.

This document might seem tedious, but if well crafted, it will open doors to further your new business. Making mistakes in this document can cause investors stay away from your business (Apex Capital Corp, 2021). The right business plan helps you navigate the day-to-day activities of your organization while focusing on the future. It will assist you in determining the strengths of your company, the competition in the market, the future of your business, and how to achieve continual growth. This will need to be updated several times a year.

WRITING YOUR PLAN

Although all business plans should be unique, it is helpful to follow a certain formula. You can purchase software to help create a business plan but be sure it is easy to understand. Look at the business plans of other successful companies when writing down your company goals. This can help you craft goals your own goals.

Below are some essential things to include in your truck business plan.

The Executive Summary

The executive summary should appear first in your business plan. However, you should only write this section when you have carefully thought about all the other parts of your business plan. In most plans, an executive summary is a one- or two-page overview of the business. Your company mission, services, products, financial information, future, and performance highlights need to be in the executive summary.

The summary should be fully accurate, succinct, and informative. If potential investors do not find your executive summary interesting, they will not read the complete document.

The Company Description

In this portion of the business plan, give details concerning the company background and history. Ensure that you describe the mission of your business. You should also explain why this new business is going to be unique from any others in the market. This section has the most important facts about your business. Some of the details that should be included are the name(s) of the owner(s), the year it was founded, location, company registration, and the number of employees. Also include details of the new customers, recent achievements, or fleet expansions.

Funding Request

Most new companies need funding from financial institutions. When you seek out investors, they will ask for a business plan to judge whether they want to invest in your company. In a funding request section, explain to the investors how much funding you need to get the company to its next stage. Financial institutions need to understand the details of company expenditures and the other avenues of income. Explain in detail why you need the money for your expenses. In trucking transportation, most of the money goes to overhead expenses, equipment acquisitions, workers' salaries, and office rent.

Investors want to know that their capital is in the best and most reliable hands, and they want assurance of a return on their investment. These institutions have seen many business plans before, so ensure that you do not make mistakes in this section (Lavinsky, n.d).

Services

Trucking businesses offer different services to consumers. In your business plan, you need to outline the services your company specializes in. This section should explain how you are going to meet the demands of your customers. Indicate why your company is needed to meet demands in your chosen market. You can also include the details about the prices of your services.

The Management Team

You need to include information about your management team (Business Plan Template.com, 2021). The founder's experience is the most important company asset, in addition to his team. For each of the members of the management team, list names, education, and previous experience. Companies that are founded by experienced and well-trained professionals have better success in the market, and any potential investors will want to know these details.

The Market Analysis

For the market analysis, your goal is to show everyone how much you understand the trucking business. When investors read your market analysis, they should see that you understand target markets, customer needs, government regulations, and industry trends. Do not take the market analysis section for granted. Do your research and include the following:

- **An outlook and description of the industry**: explain your segment in competitive trucking. Name the most successful carriers and shippers and what experts are prediction for the future of the industry.
- **The target market**: What area is your company going to specialize in? What is the size of your target market? Who are your proposed clients and what are they looking for?
- **Your distinguishing characteristics**: Thoroughly explain the needs of your future customers. How do you plan to meet the demands of these customers?
- **Pricing and margin targets**: How is your organization going to price its services? What will the profit margins be? Will you provide discounts for your future clients?
- **Market share:** How much of the market do you plan on controlling? How do you plan to get there? Where will this take your business in the future?
- **Regulatory restriction**: The government has numerous regulations concerning the transport industry. Explain how they will affect your business. How will you navigate future restrictions?
- **Competitive analysis**: This part should show that you have done your homework concerning competition. Who are your competitors? What are their strengths and weaknesses? Why is your company better? How will future competition affect

your business? Preparing to deal with the competition when the business is still new gives you an upper hand in the market. Show investors you can handle competition (Tafs, 2020).

Sales and Marketing

The next segment in the business plan looks at sales and marketing. After you have carefully analyzed the truck business market, investors want to know how you plan to acquire an excellent market share. There are two major categories in the sales and marketing section:

The company marketing strategies: In this category, explain all the methods required to gain more loyal customers. How will you promote your trucking business? Take time to explain each strategy to your potential investors. If your strategy requires major purchases or acquisitions, indicate this in your business plan. Discuss all the regions where you plan to promote your business

The sales strategy: Here, you must describe the vision of your sales. Is your organization planning to have independent sales agents or associates? How is your organization going to identify prospects in the market? Investors should know the sales closing rate.

Your sales and marketing strategies determine the future of your finances. Failing to research and make the right decision in this matter will cause your company to struggle during its first years in the market.

Financial Projections

Sales and marketing lead right into the finances of your business. Finance is an integral part of any business. This part of your plan should have all the financial statements of your company. Give financial information to investors and show them how your organization plans to meet its future goals using the finances allocated. According to RTS (2015), the financial projection segment will only be complete when you include information about cash flow, sales forecast, your organization's bank balances, and profit and losses. Explain how your business will perform and grow in at least five years using the financial projections. Remember, the projections you make in the business plan should align with any financial request you make.

Organization

This section should include all the information about company structure. Is your new business going to be a partnership, sole proprietorship, corporation, or an LCC?

Choosing a business structure is one of the key decisions you will make. Most owner-operators are advised to incorporate their business to save money. Although this could be true, you should never rush to make decisions. Take the time to research your options, as the structure you select impacts operations, costs, and taxes.

Understanding business structures available is what leads to success in the truck business. When choosing the structure, you will consider income taxation and owner liability.

Sole-Proprietor: Sole proprietorship is one of the most common structures in the world today. As the name suggests, this type of business has but one owner. This is ideal for people who prefer managing alone.

C Corporations: In the international market, C corporations' structures are quite common. Unlike a sole proprietorship, the corporation is independent. It becomes a legal entity that is separate from its owners—which gives a certain amount of liability protection. However, this structure is more complex, and it is costly to set up compared to all other business structures. This type of business must comply with numerous tax requirements and regulations.

S Corporations: In recent times, S corporations have gained popularity. These corporations are more appealing to new small business operators in the United States (Lorenz, 2014). The income and losses in an S corporation will be distributed among the shareholders in their individual tax returns. This means that you will only have to pay one level of federal taxes.

Limited Liability Company (LLC's): Most truck business owners have chosen this type of structure because of their benefits. With an LLC, business owners are given liability protection, and you do not have to worry about double taxation. The loss and profits from these businesses is passed to the owners of the institution. Each company shareholder is taxed on his or her personal returns. When the LLC has only one member, the business structure will be taxed just like a sole proprietor business. If you select this business structure, you must file articles of organization in your state. In some states, you will have to file an operating agreement to establish your business (Motor Carrier HQ, 2020).

Regardless of the structure you select for your new business, you need to know that there will be changes in law from time to time. Ensure that you are working with a structure that gives you the most benefits but stay informed on all changing laws.

SUPPORTING DOCUMENTS

Conclude your business plan by giving your investors several supporting documents. This includes copies of credit reports, tax reports, contracts, any lease agreements, resumes, and mortgage statements. This part of your business plan is not mandatory, but it will help investors and lenders to make a major decision about your business.

Financial experts say that a business plan is like a road map to a successful business. The right document will lead you to achieve your business goals by acting as a reference to everyone working in the company. Creating a great business plan takes time, but this work helps you accelerate the growth of your business.

CHAPTER 4
STEP FOUR: GET YOUR DUCKS IN A ROW

There are many government regulations to navigate in the trucking industry. It has always been heavily regulated, and you must understand each requirement lest you end up on the wrong side of the law. Here is a short guide to assist you in your business.

LICENSES & REGISTRATION

Commercial Driver's License

All the drivers in your business must have valid commercial driver's licenses, commonly known as CDLs. This is a requirement for everyone who operates heavy trucks in the United States. To acquire the CDL, a driver undergoes background checks, driving tests, CDL training, and a permit exam. Drivers must prove that they are at least eighteen years of age, and if your trucks move from one state to the other, make sure that the drivers are over twenty-one years old (Jorgensen, 2019). Most states in the country have different regulations concerning CDLs. It is important to understand what is required in your state.

Unified Carrier Registration

The Unified Carrier Registration is a new system introduced to verify the active insurance coverage in the states where a truck operates. When you complete your UCR, it is paramount to use the company federal DOT number. Your motor carrier number should not be left out either. Take time to learn everything about UCR.

International Registration Plan

The IRP tag is given by a company's home state. These license plates will allow your trucks to move in all the states. These trucks can be allowed in Canadian provinces too. The IRP license should be renewed every year.

Motor Carrier Authority Number and Federal DOT

If you do not apply for these numbers, your trucks will not be able to carry cargo from one place to the other in the United States. The DOT number is important because it tracks the safety records of your company. Your compliance records are tracked using this number too. Use the MC number, known to many as an operating authority, to identify the trucking business you are operating (Jorgensen, 2019). This number helps authorities to know the kinds of items you are allowed to haul. After establishing your business, you can get these necessary numbers from FMCSA.

To get USDOT and MC numbers for your business, you will have to successfully complete the MCS-150 report. The safety certification application will be required in the process.

Standard Carrier Alpha Code

Commonly known as SCAC, the Standard Carrier Alpha Code is utilized to identify various transportation businesses. You must have the SCAC code if you are going to haul intermodal, military, international, and government loads.

File for the BOC-3 Form

If you want have interstate operating authority, register an updated BOC-3 form. The form is registered with FMCSA, and it designates an individual in every state where your business is operating. This person serves as the processing agent for your company.

A LOOK AT TAXES IN THE TRUCKING INDUSTRY

One of the greatest problems facing trucking operations is taxes. Business owners in the industry can have a tough time understanding tax issues. As an employee, your taxes were withdrawn from the paycheck automatically. As an owner, however, you need to calculate and pay the taxes to the federal and state agencies. You must know how your new business is going to be taxed when starting your business. Before the end of every quarter, it is paramount to make some estimated tax payments. Twenty to thirty percent of the company's net earnings should be paid as tax. This way, you avoid surprises every April. When handling your taxes, you need proper planning and excellent record keeping. This information will make those tasks easier.

Types of Taxes

There are two major types of taxes you will need to be aware of.

- **Federal and state income tax**: These are calculated using your tax returns. from your salary. Business owners are held responsible for estimating and paying these taxes to the right agencies (Truck Stop, 2021).
- **Self-employment taxes:** The self-employment taxes are like the Medicare and Social Security taxes paid when people are employed. The IRS states that the tax rate for self-employment is 15.3%.

Minimize Your Taxes

If you want to reduce your taxes seek help from a professional who specializes in tax issues for trucking companies and owner-operators. The market is full of professionals who claim to know about tax activities. You can try to save some tax-free funds by contributing to institutions such as SEP, 401k, and IRA. The amount of money you send to these institutions will remain tax-free until the time you start to withdraw (Truck Stop, 2021).

Also, ensure that you keep track of your personal vehicle miles. While it is not possible to deduct the mileage from your personal vehicle, you can deduct the trips you make to various places such as the bank for the sake of your business.

If you are a parent, your children can help lower your taxes. Adolescent children can be on the payroll. If one of the children is paid $4,000 per year, they will not pay taxes on it. You will not pay taxes on the money paid to your children. The children on the payroll should, however, be doing some proper work in the company. Train them to perform simple duties such as data entry, filing, and faxing. Also, if you are paying tuition in any recognized educational institution, you can make claims for yourself or the children.

Ordinary Tax Deductions for Owner-Operators

Here is a list of deductions that owner operators can claim:

- start-up costs
- interest paid on business loans
- truck lease
- home office

- insurance premiums
- accounting services
- retirement plans
- supplies
- travel
- depreciable property
- communication equipment
- permit and license fees
- truck repairs and accessories

Learn About the Heavy Use Tax Regulations

In the United States, all trucks weighing over 55,000 pounds are subjected to the heavy highway vehicle tax. You should file and complete the 2290 tax form. The IRS publishes the form annually.

Get the International Fuel Tax Agreement Decal

This agreement was created to simplify reporting surrounding fuel utilization by heavy trucks in the United States and Canadian provinces. The IFTA agreement allows your organization to have just one fuel license (Fuel Loyal, 2017). You must file your fuel use tax four times a year.

Important tips to keep in mind

- Keep a record that supports all the deductions claimed in your tax returns.

- Label and save all expenditure receipts. Do this by maintaining a clear expense log and updating it when you are done with every run.
- Avoid overspending on company equipment, supplies, and other services to accumulate more total deductions. Remember that only a small portion of the expenses will be considered during tax filing.

INSURANCE GUIDE FOR YOUR TRUCKING BUSINESS

All businesses have different insurance needs. Each specific policy is designed to address risks in your truck business. Regardless of the number of trucks you have, insurance cover will safeguard you, the vehicles, and business.

Commercial Truck Insurance

Commercial Truck Insurance comprises several insurance auto policies for trucking needs. This policy, according to Wescott (2019), starts with the primary liability. Primary liability insurance is mandatory when acquiring trucking licenses. The aim of these policies is to protect individuals and properties from any damages brought by your business trucks.

Drivers who plan to drive their trucks on their own authority need primary liability insurance. For the business owners in the trucking industry, it is essential to expand your trucking insurance for general liability. For your trucks to remain on the US roads, you must acquire general liability.

The primary insurance policy is designed to cover for damages your truck causes to other vehicles or people when an accident occurs. With this policy, you can be sure that the public is safe. With general liability, however, you will have access to several other protections, especially during lawsuits or claims concerning your business. Insurance experts advise people to get general liability commercial trucking policies for their business. Most trucks will need at least $750,000 for insurance cover. The FMCSA will need some trucking operations to determine general liability coverage (Apex Capital, 2016).

What the Commercial Truck Insurance Covers

If you chose the general liability commercial truck policy for your business, you would be well covered in the following situations:

1. **Bodily Injuries**: When someone is hurt by one of your trucks, this insurance will pay for all medical bills. If there are lawsuits, the insurance will cover the costs that arise. It will cover people who slip and fall when inside your premises.

2. **Damaged commodities or properties**: Sometimes your truck might damage other people's property. This plan will cover the costs to fix the damage or replace properties. The policy will also cover the expenses when goods are taken to the wrong destinations (Top Mark funding, 2019).

3. **Accidents at the delivery locations:** If your driver damages items in different locations, your general liability coverage will pay for the costs incurred.

4. **False advertising claims, slender and libel**: When conducting advertising campaigns for your brand or encountering slander or false advert lawsuits, general liability insurance will help.

Additional Types of Commercial Truck Insurance

Apart from primary liability and general liability insurance, there are several types of commercial truck insurance on the market.

- **Physical Damage Coverage**: When an accident occurs, the physical damage coverage will cover all the damages in your truck. The policy covers your company equipment when disasters happen.
- **Motor Truck Cargo Insurance:** in the trucking business disasters, getting stranded, or accidents can all damage cargo. The motor truck cargo insurance ensures that your commodities are protected.
- **Bobtail Insurance Coverage:** Sometimes, accidents occur when your truck does not have a trailer attached. Getting this cover protects your trucks when they are not at work.
- **Uninsured Motorists Coverage**: Even if you carry liability insurance for your trucks, your vehicles

might get into an accident with an uninsured person. This type of insurance protects you in these instances. If you are forced to pay for the expenses of the accident from your pocket, you might end up without your business or trucks. According to recent research, one in every eight drivers on American roads is uninsured.

- **Reefer Breakdown Coverage**: Refrigerated trucks have special equipment and mechanisms to take care of. This policy is created to cover any loss of the cargo, damages of the cargo when collisions occur, and refrigerator breakdowns.

How to save on the commercial truck insurance costs

Just like all the other insurance policies in the market, it is possible to save a significant amount of money. These guidelines will help you cut down on your commercial truck insurance:

- Employ drivers who have excellent driving records
- Drive well on the road. One speeding ticket will affect the rates you get.
- Organize safe driving training sessions for all your drivers
- Try to pay all your premiums annually to enjoy great benefits.
- Increase your deductibles

- Make sure that the payments in your company are up to date
- Understand the cargo you are carrying in all your trucks

Remember, when looking for ways to save your money, do not go for cheaper policies. Cheap coverage might not give you the protection you need in your business (Wescott, 2019). Most of the time where insurance is concerned, you get what you pay for.

CHAPTER 5
STEP FIVE: ASSEMBLE YOUR FLEET

After registering your trucking business, the next process is building your fleet. Shipping cargo from one place to the other can only happen when you have the right trucks. There are many types of trucks available in the market. Choose trucks suitable for the freight you are shipping.

The process of building your fleet might be complicated when you are new in the market. Some business executives will opt to buy new trucks for their businesses while others will choose to lease. Both these processes have their advantages and disadvantages. When choosing to lease or buy, keep in mind the amount of money you have in the bank, cost of repairs, wear and tear, and downtime. Whatever option you decide, you should ensure that you are within your budget. Look for great deals when buying or leasing the trucks to save some money.

FUEL MANAGEMENT

Your trucks will only operate when they are fueled. In the United States, gas is expensive. In fact, research shows that fuel is one of the top expenses for trucking businesses. When setting up your business, if you are not careful with fuel costs, you could end up with major losses.

It is possible to control your fuel costs and increase your revenue. Fuel management is something you must learn when getting into the trucking industry. This does not simply mean finding cheap gas stations and staying away from traffic. A fuel management system can make a significant difference in your company expenditure. It is not possible to avoid gas charges, but a fuel management system helps you navigate the ins and outs of a tough situation. This technology is slowly bringing a revolution into the trucking world. Regardless of the size of your fleet, it is necessary.

TYPES OF TRUCKS

The types of freight you haul will determine the kind of trucks you need to acquire for your business. With the ideal model, you can transport machinery, livestock, produce, and equipment. If something needs to be transported by road, the right truck can deliver the job.

Australian Road Train

This type of truck is the longest road train. It can pull over one hundred trailers. The road train, however, is not very common. These trucks are only available in Australia. The Australian roads are straight, making them ideal for road trains.

Flatbed Trailer

Flatbeds are flat-level trucks without a roof or sides. The process of loading and unloading goods is quite easy using the flatbed trailer. These trucks are used to transport very heavy cargo that is not delicate. The load is secured using strong ropes or straps during transportation.

Pickup Trucks

These trucks are very common in many American households for daily activities. Parents can haul kids' gear, bicycles, and family luggage in the back when going on vacations (Lemon Bin, n.d).

Boat Haulage

In modern times, people have access to both large and small boats. You can use your large vehicle or an SUV to carry the small boats. The larger boats, however, are very heavy, and they need to be hauled using specialized boat haulage or trucks. A boat haulage is created to carry the heavy weight of a large boat.

Car Transporter Trailer

Commonly known as car carrier trailers, this double-decker or single-decker truck has several spaces created to hold vehicles in place, when moving them from one destination to the other. There are open and closed car transporter trailers in the market. Those most likely to use this type of truck are car dealerships and manufacturers.

Mobile Cranes/ Crane Trucks

Crane trucks have a fitted cable-controlled crane mounted on special crawlers. They are designed for easy and effective mobility. You will not need to assemble or set up the crane each time the truck is used.

Cement Truck

The cement truck, also known as a concrete mixer, is very common in construction companies. This truck is used to transport and mix water and cement then pour it into the right places.

Reefers / Chiller Trucks

Reefers are special refrigerator trucks. These trucks have cooling devices used to keep any supplies fresh during transportation. Reefer trucks are ideal for transporting meat, fruits, and fish.

Tow Truck

Popularly known as a wrecker, the tow truck moves impounded, disabled, wrongly parked, or indisposed vehicles. This truck is used when car owners break the law, during accidents, or when vehicles damage infrastructures. It is vastly different from the car trailer.

Furniture Truck

These trucks are designed to load and offload furniture, and most of them have a lift gate. They are used residentially and commercially for families and companies that need to haul furniture from one location to another. Although the trucks are not too strong and sturdy, they serve an essential purpose in the market.

Highway Maintenance Trucks

Highway repair trucks have some incredible features. These trucks are designed to allow a professional to safely stand on the back (Cottingham, n.a). These trucks are essential when the roads are under repair.

Livestock Trucks

Animals can only be moved from one place to the other using livestock trucks. These vehicles have special designs to ensure that livestock is secure during transportation. The best livestock trucks have special equipment to ensure that the animals are also fed during transit. They are open on the top or back to give the animals light and air.

Logging Trucks

Logging trucks are used to carry timber. They have discrete tractor units to spread out the load. Because the timber industry has grown significantly over the years, these trucks are always in high demand.

Snowplows

These trucks are used to remove snow on the roads. They can remove snow on any outdoor surface easily.

Tipper Trucks

Also known as a dump truck, these are used to transport any loose materials such as gravel, sand, or demolition rubble. You will find dump trucks on construction sites because they are needed to transport raw materials.

Trailer Trucks

In the United States, trailer trucks are used to move heavy items over long distances. These trucks can carry different cargo without issues.

Tankers

Tankers are designed to transport liquefied materials like gasoline, fertilizers, oil, water, or pesticides. The containers in this truck are insulated and well pressurized to keep the material safe during transportation. It is not easy to drive the trucks, and the trucks are considered extremely dangerous on the roads too.

Box Truck

The box truck has cuboid-shaped cargo. These trucks have several cabinets separated from the haul, and most of them have a garage door. People use these trucks to transport furniture or any other home appliance.

BUYING VS LEASING

One of the toughest decisions truck business owners must make is whether to purchase or lease their fleet. Before making your decision, you must consider several factors. Financial considerations are not the only factor in the truck business. It is paramount to put in mind the routes you will be using, organizational preference, seasonality, and types of operation in your business.

You can choose to own or lease your trucks depending on your company's needs. Before deciding, you need to understand the pros and cons of leasing and owning. It is also paramount to understand the sunshine rule, fresh wrinkle, and speedy obsolescence. When you understand these rules, it will be easier to make a good decision for your business.

Sunshine Rule

Apart from the new taxation laws, there are new accounting regulations that you need to know when making all your leasing and purchasing decisions. Business owners in the truck business will have to understand the new Financial Accounting Standard Board regulations. The sunshine regulation has been introduced to make the transaction in the leasing department transparent. All the equipment leased to clients for a period of twelve months should be correctly reported.

Speedy Obsolescence

In modern times, finance experts say that equipment gets obsolete extremely fast. Truck technology is already here, and it is pushing more business owners into leasing. People have begun to realize that they do not need to own several types of trucks for their fleet. When leasing, you can easily avoid getting into the lows and highs that come with the numerous maintenance costs (Cullen, 2018). A leasing company handles these highs and lows for you. Then you can concentrate on other important things.

WHEN YOU DECIDE TO BUY

One of the first questions many new businesses face is whether to buy an old or new truck for their business. This decision is typically determined by the amount of money the business executive is willing to spend.

Advantages of Purchasing New Trucks

- **Longer Warranty:** In the United States, most new trucks will have an extensive warranty that covers all damages—which brings peace of mind. You will also save money in repairs and damages with a new truck.
- **Known History:** When you buy a new truck, you know the history of the truck. With used vehicles, you can never know everything. It will be difficult to know how the previous owner maintained the vehicle. The new truck gives you total control of your new equipment. When you understand how to take care of the new truck, you will enjoy its services for a long time.
- **Long Term Savings:** Although buying new trucks is a very costly affair, it is a straightforward way of avoiding urgent, costly repairs in the near future (Forrest, n.d).

Buying New

Buying a new truck is a major investment, so it is essential to do some research before you make the purchase. This simple process can make all the difference in your investment. With careful consideration, you can get the ideal truck that suits all your company's needs. Here are some of the essential factors to consider when purchasing a truck.

- **What is the Purpose of the Truck?** This should be the foremost thing to remember when choosing your truck. Eliminate all the trucks that will not solve your transport needs. There are different types of trucks for various needs in the market. For example, if you plan to haul cargo, you should get a truck that transports your goods safely (Pro-line Trailers, n. d). Most trucks are designed to fit some special needs in the market. You should only buy trailers that assist your company in achieving its mission.

- **What is the Weight of Your Cargo?** The weight of your cargo is an important factor because it places a lot of strain on your vehicle and trying to pull too much puts your drivers and other road users at risk. To navigate the challenge, try to look for trucks that can carry *more* weight than what you need. This way, you will protect your trailer and drivers (Pro-line Trailers, n. d).

- **Can the Truck Tow the Trailer?** You need to know if the truck will be able to tow a loaded trailer. Failing to understand the abilities of your new tow vehicles can cause you untold misery. Small engines are not meant to tow heavy cargo. While some small trucks in the market are designed for towing heavy trailers with several modifications, you should purchase small engine trucks only if you are dealing with small weight loads.

- **What is the Truck's Braking Power?** Apart from understanding the towing abilities of your truck, it is paramount to check the stopping power. Remember that trailers carrying heavy goods take long distances to stop. The truck you are about to purchase should not have trouble when braking. The safety of your drivers, cargo, and trailer should be given top priority.

Advantages of Purchasing Used Trucks

New trucks can be too costly for individuals who are entering the market for the first time. These professionals can lack enough resources to start their businesses, let alone purchasing new, expensive trucks. For these individuals, buying used trucks is a great option. This option is currently very popular among owner-operators.

- **Less Commitment:** If you want to change your business later, investing less money with a used truck may save you from a loss on investment.
- **Cheaper Option**: Because these trucks have already depreciated in value, they typically cost less. This is an excellent option for people who want to spend less money. You can get a used truck with as little as twenty thousand dollars.
- **More Power:** Many drivers in the market today will go for older trucks. These drivers believe that older trucks have better power because they are more well-built compared to new ones.

Purchasing a Used Truck

Used trucks save new investors a lot of money. However, the truck you select should be in excellent condition. That way, you avoid spend all your profits on repairs. The low upfront costs allow you to build your fleet faster. Keep the follow guidelines in mind when you look at purchasing used.

- **Start by Performing a Background, Market, and Compatibility Check (transport systems, 2020).** The used truck should be compatible with your needs and be within your budget. Higher prices do not always signify excellent quality when buying used items. Use the internet to research trucks that suit your company's needs. Ensure you understand who you are dealing with in the purchase process. The trailer you purchase must have FHWA inspection. It is also important to ask for the service records of the truck, and all replacement parts of the truck should be available during the time of purchase.
- **Carefully Check the Structural Components of the Truck.** When you inspect the used truck you plan to purchase, examine everything. Ensure you check under the trailer for damages or rust. While it is easy to deal with surface rust in a well-maintained vehicle, structural rust means that you will have a very short service life. Do not forget to check for irregular formations, cracks, or fresh welds. When you find

these, it means that the vehicle has undergone major repairs. Structural integrity is especially important in refrigerated trucks. While saving money on purchases is appealing, they can cost you money in the long run if they are not viable.

- **Check all the Lights in the Vehicle**. Ensure that the brake lights and signals work well. The electrical connections should be functioning well when you purchase the car.

- **The Brakes Should not be Faulty.** Take time to check the drums and lining. There should be no abnormal wear and tear. The ABS system and all its wires must be working properly (Transport Systems, 2020).

- **Check the Vehicle Tires.** In most cases, tires will always tell you about the condition of the truck you are about to purchase. Carefully inspect the tires for embedded objects, ample tread, or bulges. There should be no irregularities that can cause you trouble while you are driving on the roads. Check for uneven wear in the tires. Treat this as an indication that there could be a problem with the brake drums, axle, hubs, rims, or shocks. Most trailer tires are regularly rotated, making problem identification difficult. Check for center wear, shoulder wear, and cupping because they indicate poor inflation.

IF YOU CHOOSE TO LEASE

You might consider leasing your fleet as an alternative to purchasing new vehicles. Although buying trucks is a good investment strategy for some people, it might not work for others. Leasing is ideal for companies that have very strict transport schedules. If your goal is to reduce downtime, leasing is the way to go (Pilon, 2016).

Advantages of Leasing

- **Saved Money and Time on Repairs:** When leasing a fleet, you save a lot of money and time on repairs and maintenance. Regular repairs on trucks, especially those that have been on the road for a long time, can be very costly for a trucking business. Every time your leased vehicle needs repairs, you will contract a reliable organization for the job. This makes the whole process quick and very easy.
- **Fewer Upfront Costs:** The upfront costs for leasing are lower compared to the buying costs. Small businesses do not always have a lot of capital to kick start their businesses, so leasing is an option.
- **Decreased downtime:** Cost is not the only thing that matters in the transport business. When there are breakdowns along the way because of maintenance, much time is wasted. With leasing, you will reduce the number of times you fail to deliver because no

truck was available (Pilon,2016). You can avoid the frustrations of business loss when a truck breaks down.

- **Flexible Services:** Leasing gives truck business owners a lot of flexibility. You can offer more services to customers without taking on the burdens of multiple trucks.
- **Less Commitment:** When leasing, you only use the vehicle for a specific amount of time. If you are not happy about the business you are undertaking, you can terminate the contract and go for something that works better for you.

Types of Leases

Many successful business owners consider the leasing option better because of the low costs. The benefits of leasing outweigh those of purchasing. When leasing, you need to understand all the terminations and options available. There are different types of leases in the commercial industry. Here are some of the most common types.

Capital Leasing. Also known as long-term leases, capital leases are very common in the market. In long-term leases, the truck or equipment is believed to be an asset. The capital lease has its pros and cons to the business in question. The main advantage of the capital lease is that the business is seen as the owner of the equipment (Corporate Fleet Services, 2021). The vehicle, however, is a loan to your company. The value of the equipment keeps depreciating with time.

Operating Leases. The operating lease is very different from the long-term vehicle lease. These leases are short-term, and they are known to many as serve leases. Although most businesses in the world will not consider the operating lease when dealing with cars, the option is available for those who want it. In operation leases, your business is not going to undertake the ownership of the vehicle. The lease option allows businesses involved to bargain purchasing. If your business decides it wants to purchase the truck, it can use the operating lease.

Commercial Vehicle Line of Credit. This is the most preferred lease in the market. Businesses like the commercial vehicle line of credit because of the numerous benefits they enjoy. The lease is ideal for people who want to create a fleet and at the same time lease different vehicles.

Closed-End Leases. The closed lease is very simple. The lease allows a business to lease equipment for a specific time. If you agree to lease a car for three years, the lease expires at the end of the term. The customer is protected by the price of the vehicle at the end of the lease (Jones, 2019). The greatest downside of using the closed-end lease is that you pay penalties when you turn in the vehicle early or late.

Subvented Leases. The subvented lease is a special type of closed-end lease. For the subvented lease, most leasing companies offers discounts. The lease company will determine the kind of discount to give. On the downside, however, this lease is only given to people who have very high credit scores.

Open-end Leases. This is one of the best options for business owners in the truck business. With the open-end lease, you do not have to worry about the end date. The lease does not give a specific date for turning in the vehicle. This lease gives you a good time frame to return the vehicle without having to worry about penalties. The time frame differs from one organization to the other. Many people prefer this lease option because of its flexibility. The open-end lease has its downside. You are not guaranteed the specific value of the vehicle when the lease ends.

Single Payment Leases. When you choose the single payment lease, you must pay the total amount required upfront. It is possible to combine a single payment lease with the other leases. For instance, a customer can do the single payment closed-end lease. This lease is not very costly compared to the others. There is less interest to pay at the end. The only downside is the upfront payment. Most small businesses in the market do not have large amounts of money to spend.

Used leases. The used lease is not very common in the transport industry. Used car leasing, however, is a great option. It is possible to get a used car lease from leaseholders or a dealership (Jones, 2019). With this lease, the credit requirements are favorable to the parties involved, and the terms are not very strict. The insurance premiums and tax requirements are going to be low for this lease. The only disadvantage of this lease is the costly repairs that come along the way. You will be responsible for the repairs during the lease period.

Are You an Ideal Candidate for the Leasing Process?

Leasing is an excellent option for truck business owners. The process, however, is not meant for everyone. Most car leases in the American market are reserved for individuals with good credit. With poor credit, the process of leasing is going to be very tough. Those with bad credit are never allowed to take this option.

There are numerous similarities in the process of purchasing and leasing a vehicle. You should, however, never overlook differences. Always remember that the leased car does not belong to you (Carbary, 2019). You can decide to purchase the leased car when your term has ended.

Before committing yourself to the vehicle lease process, it is paramount to ask yourself the following questions:

1. How much driving am I going to do on a typical day?
2. How is my credit score? Is it high enough to make the leasing worthy?
3. How hard am I on vehicles?
4. Is it possible to keep the leased car clean and in great shape?

Keep in mind that the leased vehicle should get back to the owner in good condition. You should only leave room for ordinary wear and tear. The owner of the truck will give you the mileage limit when you start your lease. Try to follow the terms of the lease. Otherwise, you will have problems when the lease expires.

Stages in the Leasing Process.

1. You must understand your credit. If you have exceptional credit, leasing will be very easy and affordable. Leasing is possible to individuals with credit challenges, but it gets tougher and expensive. If your credit score is not good, do some research about the other available options in the market.

2. Get the lease deal. Do not rush into the process of signing a deal. Take time to research companies with great deals. If you find a company with good deals and modern trucks suitable for your business, go for the lease.

3. Always negotiate the cap cost. The amount of money paid when leasing a vehicle is known as capitalized cost. Try to make sure that this price is not exaggerated. Research a lot about the market rates before you close the deal.

4. Never forget about the GAP. It is paramount to have the GAP insurance when leasing a car. This type of

insurance is essential because it protects you just in case the vehicle is stolen or totaled.

HOW TO MAINTAIN YOUR TRUCK

When you are the owner of a business in the transport industry, it is paramount to maintain your fleet. Your trucks should remain in great condition to save time on the road. With regular maintenance, your trucks will rarely get problems that cost too much money. Here are some basic ideas to help you maintain your trucks.

Change the Filter and Engine Oil Often

With clean oil, you can rest assured that your engine is lubricated and protected. It is easy for a truck's engine oil to get contaminated. The presence of debris, dust, and dirt from the environment gets into the oil, messing with the engine.

Your vehicle has a manual where you can learn about the number of times you need to change the oil. Some truck manufacturers recommend changing the oil every six months. Increase the number of times you change the oil if you frequently carry heavy cargo in your trucks. Drivers who must drive for very long periods at low speeds should change the oil more. When the roads are dusty, do not wait for six months to change the oil.

As you change the engine oil, it is paramount to remember that the engine needs some clear air. The oil filter should never be forgotten. When you change the filter, you remove all the debris and dust that slows the engine's efficiency. When you change the engine oil and filter regularly, you avoid serious repairs.

Inspect the Fluid Levels of Your Car Regularly

Engine oil is not the only important fluid in your truck. The engine coolant, brake fluid, power steering fluids, and windshield washer fluid should be checked (Deacetis, n.d). Engine coolant helps to make sure that your truck engines will perform better. You will avoid problems that come due to extreme temperatures.

Ignoring the power steering fluid invites problems into your business. This fluid is always termed as the hydraulic fluid. The power steering fluid helps to move several components in the vehicle steering system. The simple process of changing this fluid will prolong other expensive components found in the power steering.

Not many people are keen on the windshield washer fluid. Checking this fluid regularly should always be part of your regular car maintenance plan. It is easy for smears and dust to accumulate on the windshield. This makes it difficult for your driver to see the road. Also, when the windshield is clean, it will not get damaged as easily.

The brake fluid is among the hydraulic fluids in your truck. With time, the brake fluid absorbs moisture from the air. This causes the fluid to stop working effectively. The brake fluid must be changed regularly.

Rotate the Tires

Rotating the truck tires is very important if you want to maintain even treadwear on all the tires. This practice helps to prolong the lifespan of said tires and the truck as a whole. Rotating the tires can also assist in improving the gas mileage. During the process, the technician can identify other problems before they become costly or severe.

Cleaning the Exterior

Your truck needs to be cleaned for various reasons. Apart from making the vehicle shine, cleaning ensures that the paint is protected (Deacetis, n.d). Cleaning removes all the dust and abrasive dirt, securing the paint for a longer time. During winter, snow can affect the paint on the vehicles. The salt and sand found on the roads builds up very fast during winter, damaging paint in various areas of the truck. During the cleaning, take your time to check the undercarriage.

Take the Truck for Inspection

Every year, you must take your truck for inspection. During the inspection, a qualified professional analyzes your truck to make sure that it is in the best condition. Everyone wants to catch any safety or mechanical issues in their truck early enough. Taking the truck for the physical inspection might feel inconvenient. This routine, however, is one of the best ways of making sure that your truck lasts for a long time. The process saves you money as well.

CHAPTER 6
STEP SIX: SECURE FINANCING

E veryone wants to know how much money they need to start their trucking business. It is not so simple to determine the total funds required for the whole process. It will always vary from one organization to the other. The state you live in also determines the costs involved. The cost of your new business will be affected by the type of company you are starting, the cargo you intend to haul, your insurance coverage, the fleet you build, and the operations in the business. However, most small businesses in trucking transportation require $10,000 to $20,000 to keep everything going.

REGISTRATION & STARTUP COSTS

There are some fixed costs when setting up a new business. These costs are unavoidable.

- **DOT Number:** The DOT number is one of the most important things when starting your truck business, and currently, it costs $300.
- **Unified Carrier Registration:** In most parts of the country, the UCR fee for two trucks is currently $69 (Rodela, 2018). For three to five trucks, your company will have to pay $206.
- **Business Registration:** Registering your new business is mandatory in the United States. Each state has different costs concerning business registration. Your company should budget at least $500 for this.
- **Building Your Fleet:** The amount of money used in building the fleet is determined by several factors. If you are buying the trucks, are you buying new or used? Are you choosing to lease instead of buy?
- **Getting Insurance:** Your truck insurance is one of the most crucial costs of your business. The cost of your insurance is determined by several factors—age of the trucks, location of the truck, and commodities hauled.
- **CDL License Endorsements:** If your company deals with hazardous cargo, you will need some unique endorsements in the CDL (Rodela, 2018).

ONGOING COSTS OF RUNNING YOUR NEW TRUCK BUSINESS

When you have been given the go ahead to operate your business, you will inevitably encounter more costs along the way. Apart from the permits you got from different institutions, you will need to spare some money for daily operations. Understand these variable costs. Then, you can set the right budget for your company early.

Variable Costs

These are the costs that keep changing as you operate the truck business. Some of these costs include maintenance, meals, repairs, fuel, and lodging. Do not expect to make profits without having to spend some money on your workers and trucks. Budgeting for variable costs is always a challenge in the beginning. A few months into the business, however, you will get a feel for the right amounts and budget well.

Fixed Costs

These expenses occur consistently (Apex Corp, n. d). Some of these include the biweekly payroll, monthly insurance, and monthly fuel/maintenance costs, among others. You can budget for these costs easily because you pay a similar amount every month.

Cost Per Mile

CPM is the amount of money you must use for every mile you drive your trucks. To calculate CPM, you need to know the number of miles you drive and your costs. When you have this cost, you will be able to calculate the freight rates to make some profits from your business.

Operating Ratio

The operating ratio is what helps you understand whether you are making losses of profits. You get the operating ratio when you divide all your expenses by the total revenue.

LOANS

Funding is one of the major challenges faced by professionals in the business world. Many people have unique business ideas, but they never get to celebrate their success because of funding. Even if you can save up some money to start your business, with time you may need to expand the business, purchase better equipment, improve your office facilities, or hire better employees. These improvements require additional money. Getting a business loan can save you a lot of stress, but do not just apply for any loan from the bank. The right type of loan helps you to grow while others may lead to bigger financial problems. Business owners in the trucking department can access several types of business loans.

Small Business Administration (SBA) Loans

Small Business Administration loans have changed the lives of many businesses in the past. The SBA has various programs that give funding to trucking organizations (Sappela, 2021). The government backs SBA loans to give small businesses better financial opportunities. Most businesses applying for SBA loans do not qualify for other conventional lending available to businesses in the market. These loans are very flexible, and you can use them for various purposes. In the trucking business, you can use the loan to acquire new equipment, expand your business, or pay for normal operational expenses.

Here are some of the available SBA loans to consider:

- **SBA Microloans:** When running a small business that needs $50,000 or less, this is the best loan program. On average, this program distributes $13,000 in loans. This money can help you in purchasing supplies, machinery, or working capital.
- **SBA 7(a) Loans:** This is one of the most popular SBA loans in the market today. When you apply for the loan, you can get up to five million dollars. The money can help your business in every department. You can acquire new equipment, purchase land, acquire other businesses, or improve your premises.
- **Veterans Advantage Loans:** The veteran advantage loans are only meant for veterans and service members. The terms of the loan are similar to

SBA7(a)loans. You will, however, have a reduced guaranty fee.

Equipment Financing

As the name suggests, the funds acquired through these loans are used to acquire business equipment—like trucks and other long-term assets. With this funding, you can break down the total cost of an expensive item into small and manageable payments (Sappela, 2021). In equipment financing, you have two options:

- **Equipment loans:** If your main goal is to keep the equipment you are purchasing for a long time, get the equipment loan. This loan allows you to make the scheduled payments towards the interest and principal balance.
- **Equipment leases:** With the equipment lease, you will be making monthly payments when using certain equipment. After completing the lease, you can decide to return the equipment in exchange for a better model. If you plan to acquire the equipment, you can pay the remaining balance. When you decide to go with leases, it is advisable to do the monthly payment option because they are affordable.

Medium-term Installment Loans

These loans allow business owners to receive some working capital that is repaid with low payments every month. Typically, you pay off these loans within one to five years. You can use the loan to do anything in your business.

Business Lines of Credit

The type of funding is very similar to the ordinary credit card (become, n. d). The lender sets a certain credit limit for the borrower. You can withdraw the amount you need on several occasions until you get to the credit limit. The business line of credit will only make its borrowers pay fees and interest on the money they borrowed. For example, if the lending institution gives you a credit line of $300,000 and you manage to use only $100,000, you will be required to pay fees and interest for the $100,000. The funds can be used for most of the business's expenses.

Short-term Business Loans

The short-term business loans must be repaid on a very short timeline. Different organizations give different timelines for these loans, but most do not go past one year. Financial experts consider this the costliest loan in the market. You should only apply for short-term loans when you are in serious need. The loans are processed very fast, meaning they can save you during emergency times.

If you have been out of the business for a long time, this might be the only option available for you. Individuals with low credit scores do not get funding easily, and this can push them to opt for short-term business loans.

BUSINESS CREDIT CARDS

Not many individuals take advantage of their business credit cards. When you are responsible with this card, it can help you get your business running. Trucking companies can significantly benefit from business credit cards. The card provides you with a revolving credit line that can be used when the company is in need. During emergencies, this card comes in handy.

Business owners should use the card responsibly by paying off the card every month. This behavior boosts your business credit score, and it gives you great access to more capital every time you are in need. As an added bonus, most business credit cards have substantial reward programs.

9 STEPS TO FINANCIAL SUCCESS

At the end of the day, nobody starts a business wanting to fail. You need a plan to overcome the numerous obstacles in the market. Once you are more comfortable with the aspect of financial planning, you will have an easier time running the business. Use this guide to grow your business and get profits.

1. Choose the Most Profitable Market Niche

You are bound to make more profits as a small business if you select a specialized niche that does not compete with the large established institutions. The process of choosing your niche is critical for financial planning. This choice will determine the kind of service you want to offer, the rates you charge, and the equipment to purchase.

2. Estimate Your Operating Costs Accurately

When developing a financial plan, you need to know all your business expenses (Rasmussen, 2021). This way, it is easier to estimate your company revenue. With the right cost estimations, you can set the ideal prices for your clients. There are fixed and variable costs of operating your business. Business owners who understand their costs create the best financial plans.

3. Reduce Costs by Using the Smart Fueling Strategy

To reduce the cost of fueling your fleet, understand the cost of fuel after taxes. In most states, the well-known International Fuel Tax Agreement governs the taxes made on fuel. This has simplified fuel tax reporting for trucks that choose to operate in various jurisdictions. You must apply for the IFTA license using your base jurisdiction.

4. Create Direct Relations with Shippers

When your business starts to experience problems shipping loads, it can be very easy to find yourself forced out of the market. You need a strategy to help you find the right shippers. When you have the right shippers in your business plan, you can be assured of a good experience. You will find them by going through the freight brokers. The freight brokers are the intermediaries, and they will help you to locate the best options. These brokers play a major role, but they do charge fees that affect your profits.

5. Use an Ideal Dispatching System

The right dispatching services will help your company find cargo. With the right dispatching services, you can manage your drivers, assign cargo, and deal with customers. The system helps with compliance issues and billing. Without a dispatching service, you will be left to look for a way to handle the responsibilities through the company offices.

It pays to have an efficient dispatching service in your truck business. This service allows you to successfully handle numerous costs at a low cost. When you choose a poor system, however, the business will struggle.

6. Check Your Customer Credit

It is paramount to work with clients who have great credit ratings. When clients have good credit records, you can rest assured that they are not likely to fail payment. You find the customer's credit by using a good credit check service. Do not commit to clients before you know their credit scores.

7. Automate Your Billing Process & Compliance Software

When you automate all your billing procedures, you save both money and time (Rasmussen, 2021). An automated billing service ensures that all fees are collected at the appropriate time. Get the best systems in the market because the cost is worth it.

Most people do not realize that compliance can be automated. When there is automation in your compliance activities, you increase your efficiency. Paying regulatory fines is not a walk in the park, and most of the fines are very costly. The paperwork required for compliance is a major challenge for most owner-operators. Investing in a compliance management system is a good way to avoid problems.

8. Set Profitable Prices

Your profitability in the trucking business is determined by your pricing. You need to give prices to clients after considering all expenses in the business. Driver compensation, fuel, software, and broker arrangements are going to cost your business. While calculating the rates to give your clients, keep in mind the costs and prices being charged by other trucking businesses and make your prices competitive.

9. Plan Cash Flow to You Sustain Your Profits

For the trucking business to operate long term, you need to carefully plan your cash flow. Shippers and brokers will make payments after fifteen to forty-five days. Your business needs an ideal cash flow management system. After all, you want to have continual cash flow. Develop a strategy that keeps you going, even when you have not received money from your clients.

When looking at the processes in the trucking business, it is easy to believe that profits will come quickly. People may assume owning a trucking outfit is an easy means of revenue. When you get into the industry, however, you will realize that things are very different. Being successful means working hard to build your business, take care of your employees, and deliver to customers. Once you understand how to balance everything, you will make your profits and enjoy the financial freedom you have been dreaming about.

CHAPTER 7
STEP SEVEN: TIME TO STAFF UP

Before you bring drivers into your organization, you need to know whether you want team or solo driving. You can only make the best decision when you know the pros and cons of each.

TEAM DRIVING

When you select team driving, your driver will have someone else in the truck. This person will stay with the driver for the duration of the trip.

Advantages of Team Driving

- **Make More Money:** When your drivers are working as a team, they will be able to remain on the road for many hours (Prime Inc, 2021). The drivers help each other when driving, meaning that the truck will travel more miles. More run time means that the company is going to get more. With solo driving, the driver rests when they get tired, reducing the run time.

- **A Companion for Long Drives:** Most of the time, the roads get very lonely. When the driver has someone in the truck for a companion, this relieves some of the tedium. Some truck drivers take their spouses with them when travelling. A friend can also tag along the drive and help you overcome the lonely moments as you make money.

Disadvantages of Team Driving

- **Disagreements:** It is not always easy to match compatible drivers. Sometimes, the drivers going out with your trucks might not get along. The drivers who do not know how to manage their expectations from co-workers will have a tough time when you choose team driving.
- **Mixed Schedules:** Trucks need to be on the road to make money. The two drivers must work together to produce a plan for showers, stops, and food. Miscommunication or a misalignment of priorities can cause loss of profit due to wasted time.

How to Build a Great Trucking Team

Team driving can cause drivers untold misery when they are not paired with individuals they like (Suburban seating and safety, 2021). Driving for long distances with the wrong mixture of personalities can be extremely dangerous for everyone.

Learn how to create a trucking team that performs to your expectations. Take time to understand the needs and preferences of your drivers. For example, do not pair a driver who smokes with one who does not. Individuals who have similar character traits can work well together. Talk to your drivers when pairing them. Create schedules that match their needs. Although time consuming, it is worth it.

SOLO DRIVING

Solo drivers are responsible for making all their decisions while on the road. These professionals are alone on the road, and this strategy has its share of pros and cons.

Advantages of Solo Driving

- **Drivers Have it all for Themselves:** Truck cabs are not very spacious, meaning that sharing is not always ideal. Some drivers struggle to share the tiny space with other workers. Those people who enjoy their personal space enjoy solo driving (Prime Inc, 2021). Solo drivers never have to worry about their personal items inside the vehicle. Whether the bed is unmade or tidy, there will be no one to judge. If the driver maintains professionalism and keeps their truck safe, everything is good to go.

- **Drivers Oversee their own Work:** With the team driving, two drivers must agree when creating their schedule. One person may drive from 4 AM -11 AM. If the driver taking this shift is not comfortable working in the early hours of the morning, they will not be happy. With the solo drive, drivers select the time that is right for them to sleep and work.

Disadvantages of Solo Driving

- **Lower earning potential:** The trucking profession is very rewarding to the drivers. When solo, however, the earning decreases significantly. These drivers will have to make stops during the night to rest. When resting, there is no way to keep the truck on the road which leads to less profit.

- **Loneliness:** Solo truck drivers are alone most times of the day. It is easy for these professionals to feel lonely and secluded from the other people in the world. Extroverted people get bored when alone. Having someone to talk to and help during busy schedules is something many people prefer.

HOW TO HIRE THE RIGHT TRUCK DRIVERS

Your transport business is likely to perform well when you bring the right drivers on board. Business owners expect to invest a lot in the most advanced technologies and vehicles. Without competent drivers, however, this investment could go to waste.

The American market is dealing with a serious driver shortage. The hiring landscape is very competitive too—making things worse for company owners. If this trend continues, experts predict that there will be a serious shortage of drivers in the United States trucking industry by the year 2028.

You can make your hiring process effective by following these tips:

Attract More Millennial Drivers

Most of the truck drivers in the United States are close to retirement. You should try and expand your hiring practices to attract the young drivers. You can do this by speaking in a voice the millennial drivers are likely to hear.

Utilize social media as one of the best marketing tools in the world at the moment. Social media can significantly assist your hiring process. The younger generation has grown up using the internet. This generation values social media because it is a platform for entertainment, communication, and career opportunities.

Streamline the hiring procedures because young people get frustrated jumping through hoops in the traditional hiring process. Take time to audit your hiring processes. Look for what steps to remove to ensure that the system favors the young people.

Include benefits that are essential to young people. Young truck drivers want to be offered great opportunities like their peers in other industries. These professionals want to have a good work-life balance. Their wellness and health are crucial aspects to consider. When you post job offers, ensure you highlight the benefits to attract more savvy workers. Revise the company benefit package to attract more millennial drivers.

Employ the New Type of Truck Drivers

There are many long-haul female drivers today. Businesses in the transportation department have started to attract more women. This could lessen the serious shortages that the industry is already dealing with (Fleet Owner, 2020). The performance of the women drivers, according to research, is very promising.

Veterans have also ventured into the world of truck driving seeking an income and stability for their families. Do not let this opportunity pass by. Consider recruiting military veterans and young professionals with adequate experience.

Highlight the Culture of Your Company

Salaries and benefits given to drivers and other staff in your organization are important. However, they are not enough alone. Drivers will prefer to work with fleets that have the most appealing cultures.

In a recent statistic, 70% of truck drivers said that they were not content with their workplace because of a lack of respect (Big Road Marketing, n.d). The same drivers said that they always felt too separated from the businesses during their time on the road. Drivers in many companies complain that they never get enough support from their employers whenever they face challenging situations.

Build a company culture that offers all drivers a great environment. This will entice many people searching for job openings. When posting the job ads, never forget to highlight the company culture.

It is Time to Advance the Benefits

For several years, driver retention has been a major concern for companies in the transportation department (Fleet Owner, 2020). Freight companies have a hard time retaining their drivers. Giving better benefits can solve the challenge in most companies. The right package should have paid time off, healthcare, and better salaries. Create a good benefit program to keep attracting and maintaining the drivers for a long time.

.   .   .

Train and Equip Your Drivers

After you have brought in new drivers, do not expect to retain them by ignoring them. Giving these professionals the satisfaction they desire is what keeps them in your company for a long time. Some companies are starting mentorship programs to help retain their new hires and integrate them into the company culture.

To retain employees, you must keep them trained and up to date on new and exciting methods and technologies. Forward thinking companies are purchasing new trucks that have better and automatic transmissions. These modern trucks have better safety features compared to the old trucks. Operating the new trucks is easier too. Acquiring these trucks makes work easier for your drivers.

Have the Best and Most Reliable Fleet Management Technology

Working for a company that has a fleet involves more than just moving the vehicles from one destination to the other. The fleet drivers must deal with both international reporting regulations and external requirements. Vehicle health maintenance and safety precautions are serious concerns.

Having an ideal technology to manage these issues in your company is one of the best ways to attract great drivers. Always choose the fleet management technology that positively impacts the experience of your fleet drivers.

CERTIFICATIONS AND REQUIREMENTS

Just like the other industries, the truck industry has processes that must be followed. Truck driving professionals drive and manage big vehicles, and if unprepared or untrained, they can be a danger to themselves and other road users. A driver should meet several certifications and requirements before they can be allowed to work (Cover Wallet, n. d). Your driver should have the following before they can join your fleet:

- **Insurance:** Different insurance companies have various requirements concerning fleet drivers. Some insurance organizations will ask that you hire drivers who have been working for over two years. Small Carriers are given these standards to safeguard the truck. Discuss all regulations from your insurance providers to understand their rules. A trusted agent will offer all the assistance you require.
- **Certifications:** Every truck driver needs a CDL. The Commercial Driver's License is a requirement in almost all states. Currently, there are several types of Commercial Driver's License. Class A, for instance, is for driving trucks that have automatic steering. There are several specialty licenses given to drivers who drive various steering systems. Check to see which ones your drivers will need.

MISTAKES TO AVOID WHEN HIRING TRUCK DRIVERS

Everyone is aware of the importance of the hiring process in any organization. Your workers make or break a company. With drivers, they hold the success of the truck industry. When selecting drivers for your company, avoid the following mistakes:

Hiring Relatives Just Because They are Familiar

It is very easy to employ people you already know. If this person is an expert in driving, you could be bringing the right candidate for the job. If you bring people into your company just because you are comfortable and familiar with them, you will suffer losses. When you hire friends or relatives, use the same criteria you have used for all the other workers.

Not Checking Your Reputation Online

Some business owners feel that they are immune and secure from social media. Negative publications on various social media pages can affect your organization for years to come. Most individuals in the global community do everything online. Things like salaries, company cultures, and services in your company should not be reviewed negatively. Try to monitor your reputation. Know what happens online (Tanke, 2016). Google your organization and read what clients and strangers say about the business.

Working with Stereotypical Drivers

The global community is diverse. Unfortunately, you do not see this reflected when looking at the trucking transportation sector. Seek out diverse workers. Hire professionals suitable for the job, regardless of their color, gender, or race. By making this change, you open yourself up to a whole new market of available workers.

Being Ashamed to be in the Trucking Industry

The people working day and night in the transport world do a great job to keep the global community operating smoothly. If these professionals decided to put down their tools, many things would come to a standstill. Some individuals hold negative stereotypes about drivers. You must help new drivers see past the negative comments and naysayers who affect the truck industry in a negative way.

HOW TO ATTRACT AND RETAIN TRUCK DRIVERS

The transport department continues to grow because of online shopping and other new practices in the world. People want to shop for their daily suppliers at the comfort of their homes. Your trucking business has a better place in the market if you retain great drivers. Attracting the right drivers, however, might not be as easy as you might have thought. With the following, the process can be smooth.

The Best Trucking Associations

There is no doubt that the American trucking industry has grown over the years. There are millions of professionals working in the industry in different positions. These people deal with numerous state and federal regulations and laws. Many associations have been created to give support to the workers of the trucking world. The aim of having the association is to offer support to owner-operators, trucking businesses, and fleet owners. This is yet another way to retain your best workers. Empower and support them. Here are some of the best trucking associations in the United States.

- **AMERICAN TRUCKING ASSOCIATIONS (ATA):** ATA is considered to be the largest trade association for professionals in the trucking industry (Top Mark Funding, 2019). Many people believe that this organization is the ideal voice for the trucking industry. Since its formation, the association has done a lot for the trucking industry.
- **OWNER-OPERATOR INDEPENDENT DRIVERS ASSOCIATION (OOIDA):** This great institution was formed in 1973. Now, the association has more than 160,000 members. OOIDA is popular because of its effective representation. They fight for the rights of the members in powerful ways.
- **TRUCKING INDUSTRY DEFENSE ASSOCIATION (TIDA):** TIDA is a non-profit organization helping professionals in the trucking

industry to stay updated. The association shares useful information with its members. TIDA began operations in 1993, and it has over 1,600 member companies.

- **NATIONAL ASSOCIATION OF SMALL TRUCKING COMPANIES (NASTC):** Created in 1989, NASTC is focused on helping small carriers in the market. This institution believes that they can help the members to grow their businesses by controlling their costs. They have managed to level the competition in marketing, giving members the chance to grow and remain significant in the freight industry.

- **NATIONAL TRUCKERS ASSOCIATION (NTA):** NTA is one of the most popular trucking associations in the United States. The platform ensures that there are ideal professional practices in the entire trucking industry. The association has managed to strengthen many trucking businesses by ensuring that they have the best services and information.

- **NATIONAL ASSOCIATION OF INDEPENDENT TRUCKERS (NAIT):** NAIT has been in the market since 1981. The platform was created to help independent small business owners. Its members benefit from the information shared on the association's website.

- **WOMEN IN TRUCKING ASSOCIATION (WIT):** Created in 2007, WIT has managed to bring so much change in the lives of women truck drivers (Top Mark Funding, 2019). The mission of the association is to increase the number of female drivers working in the industry. The company has received a lot of support from transport companies across the country.

Membership Types

There are different membership types in the above trucking associations. Before joining, you need to understand each level of membership to know which one fits you best.

- **Private Carriers:** Private carriers carry their own freight. When private carriers join associations, they are given the tools they need to make the best decisions about their fleet.
- **For-Hire Motor Carriers:** These organizations move cargo from one place to the other for compensation. The companies join associations for the resources and tools needed to grow their businesses.
- **Allied Companies:** When allied companies join the trucking associations, they stand to benefit in numerous ways (American Trucking Association, n.d). These companies serve as suppliers in the market. The associations try to ensure that these companies are connected to the best markets.

- **Moving and Storage Conference Membership:** These are non-carrier organizations created to market services and goods in the trucking world. When these companies join trucking associations, they have access to industry intelligence, the best networking, and a position whenever important association meetings are held.
- **Shippers:** Shippers are institutions that do not operate fleets. They do not have any specific supplier, and they do not have an operating motor carrier department in their structures. Shippers need to participate in trucking associations to stay informed about any new changes in the industry.

Benefits of Joining an Association

Everyone in the trucking industry should try to find an association that is ideal for them. These institutions offer you many benefits. First and foremost, trucking associations are ideal for professionals in the industry because they offer you a lot of information. These organizations make sure that their members receive pertinent information concerning new regulations. If discussions are ongoing about a certain topic in the trucking industry, these institutions will inform you. Associations communicate with their members in different ways (Manitoba Trucking Association, 2021). Email distributions, monthly newsletters, and eBulletins ensure that all members are updated in a timely manner about the activities in the market.

Another benefit is the training offered and organized by some of the above organizations. Along with training, of course, come networking opportunities. This is one of the greatest benefits of joining associations. The right trucking associations provide a platform that allows you to meet new people in the same industry. It is easy to meet shippers and other professionals who will help your business through the events organized by trucking associations.

Finally, is the opportunity to further your business. It is possible to advertise your company through professional associations in the trucking industry. The institutions always ensure that their members have some of the best connections in the market.

SAFETY FOR TRUCK OPERATORS

Many people believe that the truck business is a simple and safe job for everyone. As you get familiar with the industry, however, you will realize that there is more to it. Once you manage to hire and retain the right staff, you must ensure their safety on a daily basis. Loading trucks and getting into the driver's seat is not the only physical activity that drivers face on a typical workday. This industry has some complex elements that everyone needs to understand before they get into it (Apex Capital Corp, 2016). Safety in the business is paramount. Statistics done in 2016 shows that truck driving is among some the most dangerous professions. Many workers in this industry die over the course of their careers. If you adhere to safety precautions, you will be able to avoid many of the pitfalls with this job.

Various agencies regulate the transport industries. When drivers are using the public highways, they must follow the rules and strict regulations laid by the famous Department of Transportation. When you get into the trucking business, take time to understand the DOT rules (American Team Managers Insurance Services, 2020). Truck drivers and other staff must always adhere to the Occupational Safety and Health Organization rules. OSHA regulations are meant to ensure the safety of everyone in the warehouses, construction sites, rigs, and docks where drivers visit whenever they are picking up or dropping off their freight.

There are several smaller agencies within DOT. The well-known Federal Motor Carrier Safety Administration is an agency created to reduce injuries, fatalities, and crashes involving buses and trucks. FMCSA has introduced various safety standards for everyone in the industry. When followed perfectly, the safety rules play a major role in reducing truck and bus accidents. Here are some of the most important rules from FMCSA:

- **Ensure that trucks are well maintained.** Business owners must take their trucks for routine inspection, maintenance, and repairs before every long trip. The driver should ensure that their horns, engine health, mirrors, brakes, and fluid levels are in the ideal condition. Vehicles with any problems should not operate in the general population.

- **Handle hazardous materials and cargo perfectly.** When on the road, it is very easy for cargo to move if it has not been loaded well. Each truck load should be balanced and secured. This way, it does not give your drivers a hard time on the road. Unbalanced loads are the leading cause of fatalities among drivers. The unsecured load causes the truck to overturn, causing injuries to the occupants of the vehicle and other road users.

- **Ensure that you avoid fatigue.** Drivers in the trucking industry are paid according to the miles traveled. Most of them are tempted to push themselves just to get the money fast and move on to the next job. Every driver should rest according to the DOT requirements. Late-night operations are not the best for your drivers.

Understanding safety is the greatest secret to being successful in the business. Serious companies are keen to make sure that their drivers and members of staff are safe as they move cargo from one destination to the other. Remind your drivers about the safety regulations all the time.

ESSENTIAL SAFETY RECOMMENDATIONS

Regardless of the type of trucking company you have started, it is paramount to come up with some safety recommendations for your team. The cost of truck accidents, according to recent research, is very high compared to other accidents in the world. In addition to the recommendations from FMCSA, here are some essential recommendations.

Have a Written Accident Prevention Plan

Telling your drivers to drive safely on the roads is not enough. Your company should devise an accident prevention plan (Shafer, 2011). Write the plan down and give a manual copy to all your drivers. Before employing your drivers, test their skills concerning road safety.

Train Your Drivers

The country is currently dealing with a serious shortage of qualified and experienced truck drivers. Do not just rely on the previous experience from the drivers. Take some time to train your drivers. Even the most experienced professionals make mistakes, so give your drivers some refresher courses occasionally. Verify that the people on your team are capable of driving trucks carefully and safely. Have an instructor on your team. This person should ride with your new drivers until they are sure that they are the best candidate for the position

Have Safety Meetings

Every month, bring your drivers together for the review of an important safety topic. This might look tiresome for your team, but it saves your business a lot of money. Focus on important things such as safety equipment, accident prevention, and fatigue management. When you can have the meetings in your company terminal, there will be excellent participation from the drivers. If some of the drivers are not able to come for the physical meetings, record the discussions. This way, everyone will learn.

Check for Any Red Flags

Let your drivers know that they should avoid risky behaviors to keep their jobs (Shafer, 2011). When you notice that one of your drivers is violating any safety rules, put them on probation. If you are receiving too many traffic violations from one driver, act. Terminate the employment of drivers when you see the red flags. Most companies in the world understand the importance of drug testing policies. For truck companies, these policies are crucial. Ensure that your business has a pre-employment drug test. Introduce random drug tests from time to time just to make sure that your drivers are sober. If a driver tests positive for drugs, they should be terminated immediately.

Investigate Accidents

Truck accidents can be prevented very easily. Whenever there is an accident involving your drivers and trucks, take time to investigate. If your driver caused the accident because they failed to follow the rules, act quickly. Retrain your drivers when they cause accidents. On some occasions, accidents will be inevitable, especially when caused by other road users. Offer refresher training courses to your drivers when there are multiple road accidents. Ensure that your team understands new changes on roads. Introduce the WCxK for those who have been involved in accidents.

Recognize Drivers who Keep up with Road Safety

It pays to recognize those who are well versed on road safety. Reward them often to boost their morale and motivate others to drive better. Anyone who reaches the quarter-million-mile stage without getting involved in an accident, should have a reward. Reward these workers during staff meetings for all to see.

Despite the challenges that come with running a truck business, it is possible to make things work. If you want to improve the operations in your fleet, you must become a great manager. When you are good at managing your people and fleet, your productivity will increase, and you will have happy customers. Your drivers will also be content.

CHAPTER 8
STEP EIGHT: BUILD AND MARKET

Several years ago, when I got into the trucking industry, I thought that making money was going to be easy. After setting up everything needed for the business, I embarked on the journey to get new customers and increase my company's revenue. The process was not as easy as I had hoped. During your first months in business, you may have a hard time identifying the right people to work with. If this happens, do not be discouraged. These challenges are normal, and they affect everyone getting into the trucking industry. With effort and determination, you can find great trucking contracts that bring revenue into your new business.

HOW TO FIND TRUCKING CONTRACTS

Entrepreneurs in the trucking world earn revenue based on the miles covered by trucks. If you want to increase your revenue, you must ensure that this process is continuous.

You can find trucking contracts by doing the following:

Understand Your Target Customers Well

The first step in building your customer base is to determine which customers you need in the business. Then, you can develop an effective plan. This essential step makes all the difference in your trucking business. You can define your ideal customers by asking the following questions:

1. Do they make timely payments?
2. Are they established shippers?
3. Do they have available recurring contracts?
4. Do they have an excellent reputation?

Never forget that identifying good customers is difficult, but retaining good customers is equally challenging. After getting clients, work hard to maintain them for years. Your customer service is what makes clients partner with you.

Use Load Boards but not Exclusively

You will be amazed by the importance of load boards in your trucking business. The load boards help you to connect to different shippers directly—without the assistance of a broker. The boards work by offering a long list where customers can choose whatever trucks they need.

Load boards are great when it comes to connecting to clients. Freight managers, however, should never depend on this alone. After the load boards get your company started, try to look for brokers who will assist you in scaling your business.

Partner with the Right Freight Brokers

Freight brokers are important people in the trucking business. These professionals will bridge the gap between shippers and truckers. When starting out in the market, you will need freight brokers to assist you. These individuals will work on your behalf to identify good contracts (Fleetroot, 2021). The right brokers will even do more for your company, including negotiating for more profitable rates.

Employ a Dispatcher for Your Business

Hiring a truck dispatch service can work wonders for your new business. The service will help your company to connect with brokers and shippers. Modern dispatchers offer a wide range of services to trucking businesses. Most of them will oversee collections, billing, and accounting.

Work with Registered Government Contractors

The government is always looking for contractors for various projects. The trucking industry receives numerous contracts from the government every year. Search for contracts from the state, federal, and local governments. Although the process of applying for these contracts might be longer, it is worth the struggle.

Prospect & Network

Getting started and established is always the most difficult. Prospecting can significantly help your trucking company to get customers. Search for all the available shippers based in your region and make a point to learn about their cargo and destinations. Visit these companies in person and introduce your services (Operfi, 2021).

Like prospecting, business consultants believe that networking is a great way of growing small businesses. Look for business executives who are in the trucking industry and form alliances. Attend events where shippers are present. Networking will help you to understand the current market trends and how you fit in. Be ready to meet and connect with new people all the time. These networks play a major role in the future of your business.

Avoid Client Concentration

Your trucking business should never rely on one certain shipper from one industry. If you start to prioritize a certain industry or organization, you are asking for problems in the future. Even when a customer pays more than others, you should never allow them to take charge of your business.

Client concentration is dangerous for your trucking business. When the client's contract expires, your business will be left with a loss of profits. Multiple customers in diverse industries ensure that your profits are always protected.

Continue to Build the Diverse Customer Base

Bringing new customers into any business is hard work. You must be ready to focus on the development of the business to get customers. Never rely on one customer to support over twenty percent of your business. You can network to build the customer base (Express Freight Finance, 2016). Be patient with the process, and you will be happy with the fruits of your labor. If you are new in the trucking industry, use the available tools online to understand the advantages of various industries. Talk to multiple customers in various industries that require freight services.

Your old customers should not be forgotten while you are busy searching for new ones. However, to diversify your profits, you need numerous customers. After identifying leads to a diverse customer base, start researching ideal options. With these clients, you are sure of a constant supply of work.

HOW TO MARKET YOUR TRUCKING BUSINESS

The global community has experienced some amazing changes in the past few decades. People have access to modern technologies, and they can get all the information they need through the internet. Consumers are more comfortable searching for products, information, and services online. Business owners who are thriving today have utilized the internet in their organizations. With a strong online presence, businesses can make more money and create a large customer base.

In the trucking sector, things are not any different. Businesses in this industry are trying to market their services online. When marketing online, trucking businesses should follow these guidelines.

Create a Company Website

You will not be successful in online marketing if your company does not have an official website. Customers need to refer to the website whenever they want a certain product or service. While creating the website, never forget to include the company's contact information. Potential customers need to reach you after learning about your business.

Having a website is not enough on its own to attract customers. Ensure that the company website is searchable. When customers are searching for products and services, they should see your company in the search results. You can achieve this by using search engine optimization methods. This way you have better chances of being found by customers. Also ensure that your website is easy to navigate for your customers. Frustrated potential customers will look elsewhere if they cannot easily find what they need with you.

Use Social Media Platforms

A few years ago, people only used social media platforms to connect with family and friends. Now, these platforms can be used to grow businesses. Your trucking business can benefit from social media networks. Create a company social media page to post updates concerning your services, products, and offers. The social media pages should have the company's contact information.

It is also important to integrate the company's social media platforms into the official website. As people are browsing through your social media pages, they will be directed to the company website. Online marketing works wonders when your organization has a strong online presence.

The Power of Email Marketing

Trucking businesses can use email marketing to grow their business and get new customers as well. Your marketing team should send regular emails to subscribed customers. Through email marketing, you inform customers about the latest deals in your business. If you are running a promotion, ensure that your customers are aware through their emails.

Blogging is Essential

Content is the new king in online marketing. By blogging, your trucking business can attract many customers in a short time. Start sharing useful information concerning your trucking business through entertaining blogs. People will be excited to read the content, and they will learn about your business. Look for different platforms where you can post content. Your official company website should always be the first place you post the blogs. Social media pages are an excellent option to post content as well.

CHAPTER 9
STEP NINE: MANAGE THE MONEY

S ometimes, running a successful trucking business is frustrating. As owners of the business, you put in hard work, stick to the tight deadlines, and wait for a (sometimes long) time to get paid. Numerous expenses can pile up during the shipping process. The trucks need fuel and maintenance, and the company staff needs to be paid on time. If you are not able to collect payments in time, everything in the company slows down.

If you want to be successful in business, cash management is mandatory. The process, however, is one of the most complicated tasks for trucking companies. You can only enjoy success when you deliver shipments on time and get invoices paid promptly.

THE BENEFITS OF MAINTAINING A POSITIVE CASH FLOW

In any business, positive cash flow is the greatest achievement (E capital freight factoring, n. d). A negative cash flow in your trucking business means that the company is spending more money than what it is making. Your trucking business will fail at the end of the day if you are not able to maintain a positive cash flow to handle day-to-day operations.

Incurring major debts, as well as slow-paying clients, can cause trouble. These issues can cause you to have a negative cash flow, making your work very frustrating. Every trucking business needs to have an effective collection process to mitigate these problems.

ACCOUNTS RECEIVABLE MANAGEMENT

When you take charge of the accounts receivable, you will avoid many problems. You will not have to keep wondering when clients will clear their invoices. Follow these steps to construct your payment procedures.

1. Develop effective business cash flow systems

After getting a new client, it is important to agree on the amount of credit your company provides. Before doing business with this customer, set a clear time limit for invoice payments, and ensure that your customers have an easy time making payments. Your invoice format should be kept simple.

Include the total amount due, taxes, and terms of payment on your invoice template. Do not forget to include the address (physical or online) that payments should be sent to.

The system you create should be able to track invoices the moment they are issued (E capital freight factoring, n. d). When the invoice is overdue, the system should let you know, and follow up when there are late payments. It is also an excellent idea to provide early payment incentives for clients. State these terms on the invoice, and you will be amazed by the outcome.

2. Issue Invoices Promptly

It is very risky to wait for too long to send an invoice to the customers. As soon as you complete the delivery, ensure that the customers receive the invoices. Do not assume that the invoice is received. Follow up on the matter to ensure that your client has the invoice in their hands.

3. Follow up on Late Payments

When you discover a late payment, make to the client. If you wait too long to follow up, your company might experience cash problems. Do not involve emotions when following up. If you struggle to remain calm and level-headed when speaking to late-paying clients, assign the follow-up responsibilities to someone else.

If you realize that a certain customer is not consistent with their payments, it is time to review the credit terms you have given them. Sometimes, it is important to ask for a COD to ensure you are covered.

COLLECTION STRATEGIES FOR TRUCKING BUSINESSES

Transport companies typically pay for all the expenses incurred when delivering cargo upfront and then wait for your payment. Your goal is to deliver cargo, send the client an invoice, and receive your payments later the same day. Unfortunately, this is not what happens in some cases. If you are lucky to get these kinds of customers, your trucking business will never have to worry about negative cash flow. Many customers, however, are known for paying their shipment suppliers late. In most cases, trucking businesses have to offer customers some repayment time to stay competitive. Allow your clients flexible payment terms (Trucking Office, 2020). The time of payment, however, should not exceed two months.

Late payments mean that your company will struggle with cash flow. Some owners borrow money to keep up with the increasing operational expenses. These problems are very common in the trucking industry, so you should not worry about them too much (Engs commercial finance, 2021). Over 65% of all small businesses in the US, according to recent research, suffer because of unpaid invoices. You can, however, change the fate of your business by doing the following:

Use an Effective Bookkeeping Software

Some small businesses find it easy and less costly to manage their income and expenditures with a simple spreadsheet. Although this is an easy path to take, it is not enough for trucking companies. Companies in this industry can benefit significantly from expense tracking solutions. With the ideal solutions, a company can generate its profit and loss statements very quickly. These software systems have useful features that connect the business to the banks, and you can access the accounts, regardless of your location. Your accounting processes become easier when you use software designed to handle your bookkeeping.

Always Check the Customer Credit Score

Do not work for customers with poor credit scores because it can be risky for your trucking business (Engs commercial finance, 2021). Whenever you acquire new customers, you need to do a thorough credit and background check. This might be tough when you are new in the business, but do not take unnecessary chances with new customers. Do not hesitate to seek information about the customer's creditworthiness.

The Power of Early Payment Incentives

Flexible payment options make your company competitive within the industry. Sometimes, your customers will extend their payment terms beyond the agreed time. To avoid this late payment, you should offer special discounts to customers who make their payments earlier. Everyone wants to reduce spending; your customers are no different. Many will pay early to save money. The goal of issuing the incentives is to reduce late payments and keep a positive cash flow.

Create and Enforce Strict Payment Policies

As you grow into your business and market, you will need to write effective policies concerning late payments. Taking this step is not always easy. If you have been borrowing money just to cover your operating expenses, it is time to create late payment policies. Be very careful when communicating these policies to the customers. If you have quality bookkeeping software, you will have space on the invoice template where you can write down the late payment policies.

Look into Freight Factoring

Freight factoring has numerous advantages to business owners in the trucking industry. With this procedure, you do not have to worry about all the office work related to accounts receivable (ecapital freight factoring, n. d). You sell your customer invoice receivables at a stated discount to a third-party. After selling these invoices, you get immediate cash to manage your operations. The third-party company issues your invoices, follows up on any late payments, and receives the money.

This process allows you to get the money earned from your business invoices and is a lifesaver because it allows you to get your payment in less than twenty-four hours. Furthermore, this process ensures that you have free credit checks on all your clients. When choosing a freight factoring company, ensure that they have your interests at heart. Go for companies that provide cost-saving services like fuel discounts. With the fuel discount cards, clients are allowed to fuel their trucks and pay later.

SUCCESSFUL DEBT COLLECTION TIPS

It is not possible to know when your customers will start making late payments, so it is important to always be prepared. With the right strategies in place, you will have fewer unpaid invoices (AWA collect, n.d). These informative tips will make your debt collection easier.

- **Establish Penalties for Late Payments:** In your initial contract, ensure that the customer understands all the terms to avoid confusion. Implement all the terms stated in the contract in case a late payment happens.
- **Write Down Everything:** When managing clients who are late with payment, make sure that you take notes during calls and meetings. Documentation helps you see which customers to keep.
- **Keep Clear Records**: When you notice that a client has not paid their invoices for more than thirty days, start to review their documents. Looking at their

history, you can determine whether the client is going to pay or not. Duplicate all the contracts, invoices, and generational information about the customers.

- **Involve a Professional Collection Agency:** Dealing with unpaid invoices can sometimes get very ugly. When the process becomes too complicated, bring in a professional from the transport collection department. These trusted professionals will ensure you receive the amount you are owed.

BUSINESS EMERGENCY FUNDS

Growing up, our parents taught us to put money aside for emergencies. This great advice from the older generation is essential in your personal and business life. All businesses, regardless of their size, should have an emergency fund. Having this money can help your business stay in operation when there are emergencies.

Why do You Need an Emergency Fund?

In the year 2020, businesses faced many obstacles—pandemic, floods, fires, and riots. These all presented massive losses for small businesses. One of the greatest lessons acquired by businesses in 2020 was the importance of an emergency fund.

When disasters strike, most people are not prepared. These natural calamities cannot be predicted, and this is why most people are caught unaware. Financial experts always advise business professionals to be ready for unforeseen emergencies. Setting up an emergency fund can save you a lot of stress.

Advantages of Having an Emergency Fund for your Business

Business owners try their best to plan the future of their businesses. Regardless of your plan, be prepared for the worst. Predicting an emergency in your business is not possible. With some money set aside, however, you can easily plan for this tough season. An emergency fund helps you in the following ways:

- **Your Business Can Still Operate:** When harsh times come in your life, you will not need to stop your operations to deal with it (Girsch-Bock, 2020). Your trucking business will pay its workers, fuel its trucks, and deal with any other operational costs required because of the emergency fund.
- **You can Rest Assured:** Business owners sleep soundly when they know that their businesses are safe in case of disasters, social unrest, and pandemics. The fund comes in handy during your worst times of life.
- **You can Keep Your Personal Savings:** When small trucking outfits face emergencies, many leaders use their personal savings to keep their establishments running. Protect your personal savings by starting a business emergency fund.

How to Create a Business Emergency Fund

In all businesses, the hardest part when creating the emergency fund is always funding the money. As a new business, this can be tough because we run on thin profit margins. Use these few steps to develop a business emergency fund:

1. **Determine how Much Money to set Aside.** You need to decide the amount of money needed in the emergency fund. Look at your records and calculate the amount of money needed to operate your business for a month. When saving, this is the figure you should have in your mind. If you happen to reach your emergency saving goals faster than expected, keep saving.

2. **Choose Where to Keep the Money.** Every business should have its own bank account—both checking and savings. After your business has grown, however, invest some of the money in the money market. You can also put some money in an account that gives you great returns but always keep some in savings.

3. **Start Depositing Money.** Create a great schedule for deposits to your savings. Follow the schedule you begin faithfully. Go with what works best for your company. You can have monthly, biweekly, or weekly deposits.

Best Practices for Managing Your Business Emergency Fund

One of the greatest things about emergency funds is that your business might never use them (Girsch-Bock, 2020). With a little work, you can create an emergency fund and maintain it well. Remember to start small. You do not need too much money to start an emergency fund. Small businesses can set aside $60 every month for the fund. When the sales of your trucking business grow, you can increase the savings. If you are having trouble saving because of the high costs of your business, try to cut down expenses. Look for affordable office spaces or work from your home to save on rent.

Save a certain percentage of your total revenue. This way, your savings grow when the revenue increases and slow when income decreases. This strategy is very effective for seasonal businesses that might have fluctuations throughout the year.

You should determine ahead of time what the emergency funds can be used to cover. Business emergencies come in different shapes and sizes. It is important to manage the amount of money you have saved when emergencies strike. Know for which events the money can be used.

SETTING YOUR RATES

There are many hidden charges in this business. Most of the time, these costs increase the cost of running your business, and if you are not careful, you might end up taking losses. It is easy to undercharge or overcharge your customers when you are not keen on your company's operational costs.

It is essential to have the latest market information concerning freight rates in mind. These rates continually fluctuate, but they can guide you to make the best decisions. In any business, the most important thing is demand and supply (Freightos, 2021). Regardless of the quickly changing rates, it is the responsibility of trucking companies to make sure that they haul cargo at the right time at an agreed upon price.

Many people know about three shipping methods: sea freight, road freight, and air freight. The cost of shipping is somewhat determined by the method chosen. In road freight alone, there are numerous factors to consider when determining the cost of shipping. Here are some of these factors:

- **Weight and Dimensions of the Cargo:** The actual weight of the cargo you are shipping is very important. The weight of the freight affects the total shipping cost. This is one of the most important factors when determining cost. The volume of the dimensions has to be determined (ProConnect Integrated Logistics, 2020).
- **Unexpected costs**: When shipping cargo, it is important to be prepared for common unexpected

costs. Some of these costs come from stolen cargo, unforeseen delays, lost items, and damaged cargo.

- **Destination of the Cargo:** The origin and final destination of the shipment affect the total shipping costs. If you are moving cargo for long distances, the costs of shipping will go higher. Furthermore, every country has its special charges when it comes to duties and taxes. There are custom duties that need to be cleared before you import or export your goods from one country to another. These costs should be included when you are calculating the costs of shipping.

- **Delivery Time and Speed:** Most of the time, this is related to the delivery method you have selected. When you select a fast delivery, you will need to pay more.

- **Value of Your Cargo:** This is among the secondary factors affecting shipment costs. When you are shipping high-value cargo, you will have to pay more. This type of cargo needs insurance to secure against damages, loss, or theft.

- **Incoterms of Your Global Sales Contract:** When people are exporting products, Incoterms play a major role in determining responsibility and expenses people have to deal with. There are 11 Incoterms, and each has various costs and liabilities. Always put these costs into consideration while determining your shipment costs.

Understand How to Create a Good Cost Per Mile

When you do not know the amount of money used in running your business, it will be difficult for you to have a cost-per-mile rate. To get the true cost per mile, you have to consider the fixed and variable costs of your business. Calculating this rate is only possible if your company maintains accurate financial reporting and bookkeeping. Every single dollar spent in the organization should be recorded. Small office expenditures should not be left out. All money spent affects the overall profits of your business.

Many companies experience problems when calculating the cost per mile because of sloppy bookkeeping. If you want your business to be different, ensure that you have accurate monthly financial statements. This statement should be well detailed to avoid confusion.

The rate you set should support your business and at the same time attract new customers. A good rate should be high enough to pay all the expenses of the business and leave some good profits (Capital Freight Factoring, n. d). Maintaining competitive rates is difficult, but it is worth it. To balance the cost per mile rate, you need to do the following:

1. Know the cost per mile you need to cover expenses.

2. Based on those expenses, set your rate to allow for a profit margin.

3. Be sure to measure your estimated rates against the competition.

Drive More Loaded Miles

Most drivers love loaded miles because it brings more income for your business. Finding ways to get additional freight and ensure the trucks are always on the move gives dispatchers, company owners, and fleet managers many a sleepless night. Small companies, established fleets, and growing companies work hard to get cargo for their trucks. Try all means to book full cargo for your trucks.

TRUTHS AND MISCONCEPTIONS REGARDING FREIGHT PRICING

The trucking and logistics market has experienced some great changes in the past few years. The legends and veterans in this market, however, still pass some of their beliefs and stories on to the modern generation. Thankfully, the new entrants in the trucking industry have gone to universities and colleges, and they have realized that the logistics and supply sector has numerous misconceptions. Here are some of the beliefs and thoughts that mislead people in this competitive market:

Bigger Volumes Equal Better Pricing and More Leverage

After working in the transport industry for several years, I have come to realize that this narrative is not true. Most shipping companies in the market will prefer to work with trucks that are capable of handling the volume of their cargo. No special pricing is given to smaller carriers who must cover several trips to carry the shipment to the final destinations. Most of the large shippers will look for the right trucks that can handle the cargo at a reasonable price.

Logistic Businesses are Better when Bigger

Many venture into the competitive freight brokerage department because they want to attain buying power and take advantage of the vast network offered by the freight brokerage market. Most of these professionals understand that bigger will not always turn out to be better in this field (inTek freight and logistics, 2021). The large logistic companies typically have the best freight prices, but this is not always the case. Even more troubling, larger companies bring capital and resources, but they also bring a serious disconnect between the provider and customers. As a logistic company grows, the top executives can get too busy making deals, leaving the daily operations of their businesses to junior workers. When this happens, the value of services deteriorates, causing clients seek services elsewhere.

Getting Your Money's Worth

People have always believed that you will get services that are worth the amount of money you are paying. Gone are the days when the price determined the quality of services and products. Paying high amounts of money does not mean that you are guaranteed excellent services. Established companies in the market charge very high rates for their services. These institutions, however, may not give you better technologies and services. Take time to search for companies that have ideal services. Your budget will determine the company you settle for. Some companies will charge fair prices and give you top-notch services.

You Must be a Strict Negotiator to Bring Prices Down

This is a very common belief among freight companies. The older generation believed that someone had to be very tough during the negotiation process to get the ideal price. Freight is always considered to be a commodity for purchasing. This narrative, however, is not true. Freight, according to the expert, is a service. People need to realize that freight prices are determined by several factors. When negotiating freight prices, it is paramount to keep in mind the market rates. Start by collecting market data to understand how other companies are charging their customers.

100% Asset Models are the Best

Everyone knows that using the one size fits all method is not effective for all companies. Logistics and freight managers need to know that diversification is important. It is time for shippers to start diversifying their supply and logistic strategies in both non-asset and asset providers. A logistic and supply chain that is well-diversified brings out the best performance with fewer risks.

FUEL MANAGEMENT PRACTICES TO ENSURE YOU OFFER COMPETITIVE PRICES

A recent paper revealed that diesel fuel is among the highest costs for the trucking business—at more than %20 of total trucking costs.

Your drivers will determine the amount of fuel your fleet is using. Research from the famous National Renewable Energy Laboratory proves that trucking companies can reduce their fuel consumption when they encourage good driving behaviors.

Setting up an ideal fleet fuel management plan can be tough in the truck industry. However, with the following tips, you will never complain about high fuel costs.

Tips for Lowering Fuel Costs

- **Observe the Speed Limits:** Many drivers believe that observing the speed limits is for their safety. This practice, however, is essential when it comes to reducing fuel consumption. Most trucks have a speed

range where it gets to the optimal fuel consumption
(Samsara, 2021). With speeds of over 50 miles in an
hour, your truck uses additional gas.

- **Encourage Safe Driving:** Distracted, erratic, and
  aggressive truck driving has a negative impact on
  your company. All these practices affect your savings
  and driver safety. Have a fleet safety program for
  your drivers. It is paramount to coach your team on
  the right driving practices. These practices ensure that
  your trucks have low wear and tear, reduced fuel
  costs, and fewer accidents.

- **Safety Inbox:** In all industries, technology has made
  operations smoother. The trucking industry has
  embraced technology too, and it is now very easy to
  track fuel-guzzling activities, when you have an
  effective fuel management system. The fuel
  management system helps you identify the best
  drivers in your fleet as well.

- **Do away with Engine Idling:** If you want to see
  significant changes in your fleet fuel consumption,
  eliminate engine idling. When idling, heavy vehicles
  consume close to one gallon per hour. In the United
  States, idling trucks consume more than one billion
  gallons annually. The best thing to do is train your
  drivers to avoid idling and prevent the losses for your
  business.

- **Fleet Maintenance:** Your trucks will operate as

intended when you take them for regular maintenance. Do not wait for the trucks to be faulty. Major repairs are usually quite costly. Check the truck tires and wheels regularly to avoid wasting fuel. Your fleet engines are paramount, so always make sure that they are functioning well. Do not expect a faulty engine to be efficient. Address all engine issues the moment they are discovered. It is safer to handle engine problems early.

- **Take the Time to Plan Your Routes:** Your trucks consume a lot of fuel when they take longer routes. The time wasted on the road can never be recovered. Start planning your routes before your trucks start their trips. When planning the trip, the ideal route should reduce the truck mileage and fuel consumption. If possible, combine trips.

- **Eco-driver Training:** If you want to achieve optimal fuel consumption, eco-driver training is helpful. Drivers should be trained on all the factors that determine truck fuel consumption (Stealth Power, 2019). Plan for events where your drivers can interact and learn how to make every gallon inside the trucks count. Award the drivers who manage to keep up with the skills they acquire during the training. Look for ways to make the drivers accountable for their actions while on the road, and you will be amazed by the results in your total fuel costs.

- **Understand Fuel Types:** Fleet managers must understand the fuels available in the market. You should be aware of the kind of fuel that suits your trucks. There are alternative sources of power and new fuels available in the American market. Choose fuel options that help preserve the environment and are affordable for your business.

CHAPTER 10
STEP TEN: EMBRACE TECHNOLOGY

Technology is one of the best things that has ever happened to small business owners. Every industry has benefited significantly from technology. The trucking industry is no different. Professionals in trucking have realized that technology is one of the best ways to maintain accountability and streamline daily operations.

Software that will monitor driver and truck performance is available, and business owners can keep all the records of their drivers' histories through these programs. Some software can even make drivers safer on the roads. Insurance companies are more favorable toward truck businesses with advanced technologies.

These insurance companies know that the risk of accidents gets lower when the best trucking systems are in place (Fleet

Owner, 2017). Let us explore some of the awesome technologies being used by drivers and owners today.

Dynamic Routing

You will need to identify the best routes for your trucks to reduce the costs of the shipping process. Dynamic routing is one of the most useful tools when identifying the routes your trucks must take. This program sends data concerning traffic and changes in weather. When you access this information in real time, you can alter the routes your trucks are taking.

Dynamic routing has helped businesses trim the excess miles. Fleet managers can identify the quickest routes when dispatching their freight and avoid too many stops with the dynamic routing. Each passing day, dynamic routing software is evolving, and it can help your business advance as well. Your clients will be happy when you deliver their shipment quickly and in good shape.

Forward-facing Cameras

Forward-facing cameras, popularly known as dash cameras, have been around for a long time. With modern technology, these cameras are improving both in quality and pricing. There are very good quality dash cameras in the market today and installing a high-quality camera system in your truck can save your company a lot of frustration.

Many truck drivers do not like forward-facing cameras because they believe that their privacy is being invaded. The benefits of these cameras, however, are too many to ignore (Truck Pulse, 2019). The cameras can record any risky driver behavior, like drivers using their cell phones, falling asleep, or eating while on the road. This information and real-time monitoring can help prevent dangerous accidents on the road.

On the other hand, if accidents take place, you can also use the footage in the camera to defend your responsible drivers who were following policies correctly. The footage can then be used to determine the driver who is at fault.

You can also use footage from your trucks' cameras to train other drivers in your fleet. New drivers who are joining your company can benefit from the footage. Explain to the new drivers how they can correct or avoid some of the dangerous behaviors recorded on camera. You will be impressed by the outcome of having an effective dash camera system. Most of your drivers will be more vigilant on the roads when they know they are being watched.

Driver Scorecards

The safety of your drivers and trucks while on the road is very important, regardless of the size of your fleet. Over the years, many technological advances have made this endeavor easier.

The driver scorecard system helps to evaluate the performance of your drivers on certain driving metrics. Every truck business owner wants to know whether their drivers are idling, speeding, or being aggressive on the roads. It is possible to measure all these metrics using GPS fleet tracking. The popular telematics system can be of great help in gathering information to help you better understand the behavior of your drivers.

When you have an effective scorecard, you easily pick out the risky drivers in your fleet. The system allows you to identify any driver who needs extra training, and it identifies your excellent drivers too. It is important to reward and motivate these professionals because they are doing a good job for your business (Fleet Owner, 2017). When you design and implement your driver scoreboard well, you will increase the efficiency of your fleet.

Collision Mitigation Technology

Many lives have been lost because of truck collisions. The large size and mass of the trucks can be partially blamed for the numerous accidents. Whenever heavy trucks collide, there is a high price to pay. The possible insurance claims, expensive lawsuits, and loss of life or equipment give business owners sleepless nights.

Installing collision mitigation technology in your fleet can help your business in many ways. This technology operates as an extra pair of eyes when drivers are on the road. Your drivers will get warnings and special information, helping them to avoid road accidents. The collision mitigation technology systems use lasers, cameras, and radar systems to identify a risky situation. Some advanced systems automatically reduce the speed of the truck to prevent accidents.

The collision mitigation system uses visual displays. Normal mirrors cannot give the view provided by the systems. Although most trucking businesses use this system to reduce accidents and create an overall safer driving experience, it also has other benefits. These systems can help you improve compliance and increase your CSA scores as well.

This modern technology is also an excellent way of reducing your insurance premiums. Many new trucks must install the collision mitigation system as a standard requirement. The system can monitor the trucks' surroundings too and notify you if the drivers are speeding.

Electronic Logging Devices

Several years ago, this was an option for commercial trucking operations. Today, however, this is one of the requirements. Your trucking business needs electronic logging devices, popularly known as ELDs. Without them, your business will face legal issues. The ELD is used to track and record the number of hours drivers are on the road. This system ensures that all drivers are not spending too many hours on the road just to make extra money. Each driver must adhere to the restrictions laid by the Federal Motor Carrier Safety Administration. Some small companies try to avoid the ELDs because they want to be on the road for many hours and increase their revenue. This, however, is not acceptable to authorities.

Trailer Tracking

Managing assets is one of the most frustrating situations business owners must do. They tend to underutilize some of them. If you want to track your company assets and manage your wear and tear, trailer tracking technology is what you need (Fleet Owner, 2017). With this modern system, you can manage how each of your company assets is being used. With ideal GPS tracking, you will know what is happening to your trailers all the time. Trailers are expensive assets in your business. Adding a tracking system to your fleet can give you peace of mind because you are sure that no one is going to steal the trucks.

Temperature Tracking

Many carriers have embraced the temperature tracking technology already. If your trucks carry fresh produce for animal and human consumption, you need a temperature tracking system. This is a mandatory requirement for fresh produce carriers currently. The system ensures that your food is well refrigerated. The vehicles must be cleaned after every load to ensure that there is no contamination, and the temperature tracking system makes sure that food is safe during the transportation period.

CHALLENGES OF THE TRUCKING INDUSTRY

Every business in the market faces its share of challenges. For those brave enough to establish their own trucking company, here are some of the challenges you can expect to encounter. Remember that having a plan ahead of time will help you deal with or circumvent the challenges as they arise.

Shortage of Drivers

American trucking transportation is dealing with a massive shortage of professional drivers. Numerous solutions have been proposed and attempted but nothing seems to be working. Drivers are leaving their jobs when they cannot agree with their employers over contract terms. Offer your drivers good compensation and benefits to retain them long term. Finding and keeping good drivers who take care of your truck and shipment is hard work.

High Fuel Costs Reduce Operational Efficiency

The cost of fuel is always fluctuating. It is always hard to predict when prices will go up or down. When the prices are too high, they affect the fleet operations in a major way. Fuel has some major effects on the environment too, and this can give companies ethical issues. Businesses in this industry can only solve fuel problems when they embrace the fuel-free systems.

Security is a Major Concern

Every new advancement comes with both advantages and disadvantages. Many trucking companies are embracing the efficiency of using high quality technology to further their business. However, you must also be aware that cyber security is more important now than ever before. This added concern is manageable, but it will also require funding to appropriately protect your assets.

TECHNOLOGY WILL BRING POSITIVE CHANGE

New technologies in the transport industry have brought a new revolution. Consumers and transport stakeholders should be prepared for more changes. Trucking companies have changed their delivery processes due to advanced technology. The positive change has not only brought more money to the table. It has also saved many lives. Here are a few trends that the trucking industry should expect in the future. It is worth researching these trends as you lay the groundwork for your new business.

Hybrid trucks

People have used gas cars for many years. However, the transport industry, is evolving every day, and hybrid-based vehicles are becoming popular. People are more interested in hybrid automobiles now than ever before because of the exceptional fuel performance. The technology used in hybrid cars will soon find its way into the trucking industry. Diesel trucks could be a relic of the past if this happens. Businesses could cut down on fuel expenditure while using hybrid technology.

Self-driving vehicles

In recent years, many vehicle manufacturing companies have promised to deliver self-driven vehicles. If self-driven trucks are introduced into the market, the industry will never be the same again. Companies will cut down on the expensive driver salaries (STT Logistic Group, n.d). If this happens, the driver shortage will no longer be an issue plaguing the trucking business.

The world has undergone massive changes in the past few decades. Technology has brought a great revolution in the way we operate our businesses. Do not be left out! Your trucking business needs technology to remain competitive in the market. Some of these technologies are very costly for new businesses, but they are worth it. The right technology ensures that everything in your business is running smoothly.

CHAPTER 11
STEP ELEVEN: FLEET MANAGEMENT 101

Your greatest responsibility as the fleet manager is to make sure that you operate your business within the budget. Every fleet manager works on reducing the costs of the business. You need to be aware when your business is making too many costly repairs, extreme payments, or experiencing poor fuel consumption. These costs determine your profits. If the costs exceed your earnings, it is time to change your strategies.

STRATEGIES FOR BETTER FLEET MANAGEMENT

The task of managing a fleet is challenging. Regardless of the size of your company, you need to be well prepared. A great manager must ensure that the cost of running the fleet is not too high, increase the efficiency and safety of the organization, and, at the end of the day, reduce liability. These responsibilities are no laughing matter. Those who have just joined the industry might have a tough road ahead. However, with the right strategies, your success is possible. Focus on the following practices, and your business will be the best.

Have Long-Term Strategies

From the start of the business, try to plan some goals for the future. Set up various processes to efficiently deal with new challenges and scale your fleet. Everyone wants to believe that they will easily adapt to growth, but you must be prepared for whatever might happen in the future. Make your systems simple so that they can be easily scaled up or down to handle your ever-changing business.

Have an Effective Vehicle Replacement Schedule

Once they hit 70,000 miles, most vehicles will not perform at optimal levels. The trucks in your business will reach these miles faster than other vehicles, and some trucks get to this mile marker in just one year. Ensure that your truck's life cycle does not go beyond four years (Azuga, 2020). Most companies prefer to lease their trucks to find the right truck life cycle. This great strategy helps your business to reduce costs on liability and repairs.

Work on Preventive Maintenance

The numerous repairs on vehicles combined with down time expenses cost your business a lot. These repairs slow the growth of your business. With preventative maintenance, you can reduce the possibility of major repairs. This also helps your business to always remain DOT compliant. Drivers sometimes benefit the most when a company prioritizes routine preventative maintenance. The vehicles will rarely get into major accidents or break down, which means less down time for your drivers and their paychecks.

Reward Good Driving Practices

When your drivers have excellent driving practices, this significantly reduces repairs, liability, numerous costs, and inefficiency. The efficient drivers in your company get into fewer accidents, use very little fuel, and rarely incur penalties. Start training your drivers to understand costs, fleet maintenance, fuel usage, and any other important thing in the business (Azuga, 2020). These individuals should be aware that they are responsible for the growth of the business. They will be rewarded when the company does well.

Have an Asset Tracking System

Most truck companies are not aware of the number of assets they have acquired. The fleet owner should always be aware of all business assets. This prevents the purchase of redundant and unnecessary equipment. If you do not know what you have, how can you use it to your benefit? With modern asset tracking, you can optimize the use of everything at your disposal and avoid theft.

Geofencing

This strategy creates a special virtual perimeter surrounding your location. With geofencing, the fleet owner gets an alert every time one of the fleet assets leaves or enters that specific location. For this reason, it is easy to know when one of your assets is operating at the wrong hours. Geofencing allows fleet managers to track any idle time among the drivers.

Optimization in the Fleet Size

At first, business owners are tempted to purchase numerous trucks. This process, however, can strain your business budgets in the end. One the other hand, when you do not have enough trucks, your business will fail to perform to your expectations (Palter, 2020). The number of vehicles should match increased workloads and unexpected truck downtimes.

AVOID FLEET MANAGEMENT PROBLEMS

When your business has a large fleet, you are going to experience more inefficiency. This is because of the many working parts of your business. It is very important to have audits from time to time, and it is important to always communicate your concerns with your drivers. There are several ways that you can avoid problems before they happen.

Create Strong Policies

Take time to document and communicate all important company policies to the members of staff. Good fleet management is possible when an organization sets very clear policies and expectations. Everyone should understand every policy in your organization. This only happens when you have excellent, ongoing communication.

Automate the Fleet Management System

Most processes are time-consuming if you do not have an effective electronic fleet management system. There are many platforms available in the market to make fleet management easy. When you do not waste time on the manual tasks, you have time to focus on the most important tasks in the company.

Act Quickly to Protect Safety

There are many safety hazards and distractions for drivers. A good fleet manager acts before the company gets into serious problems. Do not wait for accidents to happen. When you wait, your business and drivers will suffer. For example, purchase a reliable hands-free device, in-cab camera device, and an effective driver behavior app. Some managers might feel that these items are costly for the business. The cost of not having them, however, is worse (Chapman, 2017). It is necessary to know what your truck drivers are doing when their leaders are not close.

Make the System Accessible and Simple

Everyone loves to take the easy path of less resistance. Your fleet drivers will keep up with their routine vehicle maintenance and service if you make the scheduling, reporting, and inspection system effortless. Gone are the days when companies had whiteboards, file holders, and handwritten notes in the offices just to ensure that everything about the fleet was running well. Look for modern fleet management software. Automation makes a big difference.

Establish Disposal and Purchasing Guidelines

Consistency is paramount in this business. When a truck business does not have any purchasing guidelines, they will be tempted to purchase trucks and use them for a short time. When your truck business lacks knowledge and guidelines concerning the right time to purchase or dispose of equipment, it is bound to have problems in the future. Make sure that everyone is on the same page and ensure that the purchasing plan you have works for your needs

Set Purchasing Requirements

When shopping for equipment, it is possible to find very good deals. It is very important, however, to have standard equipment requirements. These requirements make your purchasing process cost-effective. Doing this is easier when the fleet manager is making all the purchases. Companies have various departments, but it is essential to assign all purchases to just one fleet manager.

Set Goals for Driver Performance

Some of your drivers may excel at their tasks. Others, however, need to be more carefully supervised. Communicate your expectations concerning the daily operations of the driver. Drivers should perform vehicle inspections when needed, achieve the right fuel efficiency, and show excellent driving performance. Reward drivers who are responsible when performing their duties.

Track and Document Everything

In business, metrics are critical—they help in monitoring the growth of your company. These metrics, however, can become ordinary numbers if you don't do your part well. If you plan to oversee company fleet operations, you must make the right measurements (Chapman, 2017). Know the accurate cost per mile, operational costs, and total costs trends in your organization. Ensure that you can easily track this data by having an effective fleet management system. Data affecting your fleet should be monitored at all times. With driver and performance data, you optimize your fleet utilization (Palter, 2020). This data helps you to make the best-informed purchases in the future. Fleet managers should track the following metrics:

- **Consumption of Fuel:** This should include the fueling days, fuel type, cost, quantity, and location.
- **Purchasing and Leasing of Equipment:** All warranty and contract information should be stored well.
- **Driver Performance:** In case of accidents or infractions, write down all information about the cause, location, and date.
- **Maintenance:** The costs, parts replaced, and repair dates need to be available for future reference.
- **Vehicle Rotation:** Record the person signing out the trucks, the date, time, and exact mileage of the trips.
- **Credentials:** Driver certificates and licensing must be documented too.

It is also time to abandon the traditional file folders. There are new, cheap ways to store your data online. Your fleet information is safer when stored in the right digital systems. Employment records, work orders, photos, invoices, product manuals, and any other useful company data need to be kept in a reliable digital location. You should be able to access this information using any internet-connected device.

Continually Educate Yourself

As a fleet manager, you should try and keep up with the ever-changing market. Look for blogs, a good industry association, and trade publications to keep track of the changes taking place. Never fear trying out the new technologies available in the market. Technology changes might look complex at first, but when you understand them, they benefit your business in numerous ways.

SOLVING FLEET MANAGEMENT PROBLEMS

You need to know you are not the only one facing the challenge of running your trucking business. These daily issues affect all fleet managers. Fortunately, you have some tricks to make your daily operations easier and simple.

AFTERWORD

Running a business is not a job for everyone. Businesses challenge everyone, even the most prepared people. Prepare yourself early for the competitive business industry to enjoy the benefits of being an independent truck business owner. The trucking business will give you the following benefits:

- **Freedom:** As an employee, you must work according to the rules set by your employer. This does not happen in the trucking business. You will always be at liberty to select the routes you want in order to earn more income. The business gives you the freedom to work with your own flexible schedule.
- **Pride:** Many in the United States dream about owning a business. It can be compared to buying a house. When you own a property, you get to choose

the colors you want for your walls and many other things. As a business owner, you enjoy similar benefits. If you are disciplined in your activities, you can do whatever you want regarding your business.

- **Success:** The global community is still in the process of recovering from the pandemic (Motor Carrier HQ, 2020). People have lost jobs because of the disease. To find financial freedom, consumers need to invest in growing industries. The trucking sector happens to be one of the best places to invest your money. The best thing about the business is the fact that you do not need much to start. Years later, it is easy to sell your trucking business at a profit.

The field is tough. Even when you have all the expertise in the world, you will take losses if you do not have discipline. Most of the financial and logistic operations of the trucking business can be overwhelming, and they can give you trouble if you do not manage them properly. Most owner-operators must deal with rising costs, very rough competition, heavy regulations, and fluctuating markets.

In the presence of all these hardships, however, financial experts believe that the trucking sector is one of the most important services in the American market. The industry has been able to overcome various economic crises, changing technologies, international pandemics, and environmental regulations. In the coming years, this industry will remain essential (Capital Freight Factoring, n. d). The numerous opportunities for growth in the truck business are what make this department worth the struggle. If you put in more work, operate with exceedingly high efficiency, and work smart, there will be major rewards in the end.

Trucking companies play a particularly important role in the American economy. The trucks ensure that essential products are delivered at the right time. This is the best time to start the trucking business you have been dreaming about. Creating a successful trucking business is not as complicated as most people believe.

Starting and maintaining a successful trucking business is one of the best ways of earning a high income in modern times. Hopefully, we have equipped you with enough knowledge to go out there and create a successful trucking business on your own! Good luck on your journey!

Thank you for choosing this book. If you have enjoyed this book or found it to be helpful, please consider leaving a review on Amazon.

To go directly to the review page, you can:

- Scan the QR-code below with the camera on your phone
- Or type in the Shorturl link above the QR-code in your internet browser

shorturl.at/TUPWZ

Thank you! We appreciate your support!

REFERENCES

American Team Managers Insurance Services. (n.d.). *The most important safety rules for trucking operations*. Retrieved October 16, 2021, from https://www.atminsurance.com/the-most-important-safety-rules-for-trucking-operations

Apex Capital. (2016, May17). *Safety regulations for trucking companies*. Retrieved October 16, 2021, from https://www.apexcapitalcorp.com/blog/safety-regulations/

Apex Capital. (2016, April 19). *Motor carrier insurance requirements*. Retrieved October 18, 2021, from https://www.apexcapitalcorp.com/blog/trucking-insurance/

Apex Whitepapers. (n.d.). *How to write a business plan for your trucking company*. Retrieved October 17, 2021, from https://www.apexcapitalcorp.com/whitepaper/trucking-business-plan/

Apex Capital. (n.d.). *The cost to start a trucking company.* Retrieved October, 21, 2021, from https://www. apexcapitalcorp.com/startup/cost-to-start-a-trucking-company/

ATBS. (2019, July 21). *6 Things successful trucking business owners do everyday.* Retrieved October, 21, 2021, from https://www.atbs.com/post/6-things-successful-business-owners-do-every-day

AWA. (n.d.). *Tips for successful debt collection in the transportation industry.* Retrieved November 5, 2021, from https://awcollects.com/tips-for-successful-debt-collection-in-the-transportation-industry/

Azuga. (2020, April 22). *Top 10 fleet management tips for fleets of any size.* Retrieved October 22, 2021, from https://www.azuga.com/blog/top-vehicle-fleet-management-tips-for-fleets

Become. (n.d.). *All about tracking loans.* Retrieved October 21, 2021, from https://www.become.co/loans-by-industry/trucking-business-loans/

Bison. (2015, August 4). *A day in the life of a fleet manager.* Retrieved October 15, 2021, from https://blog.bisontransport.com/2015/08/the-day-in-the-life-of-a-fleet-manager-2/

Bull Ring. (n.d.). *5 Basic maintenance tips for your truck.* Retrieved October, 21, 2021 , from https://www.bullringusa.com/5-basic-truck-maintenance-tips/

Business in Gambia. (2020, Dec 8). *4 Ways to get clients for your trucking business with online marketing.* Retrieved October 28, 2021, from https://businessingambia.com/trucking-business-with-online-marketing/

BPlans. (n.d.). *General freight trucking business plan.* Retrieved October 17, 2021, from https://www.bplans.com/general-freight-trucking-business-plan/

Carbary, Meghan. (2019, February 18). *How to lease a car: The leasing process explained.* The car connection. Retrieved October 20, 2021, from https://www.thecarconnection.com/car-loans/finance-guides/how-to-lease-a-car-the-leasing-process-explained/

Chapman, Matt. (2017, March 14). *7 Habits of highly effective fleet managers.* Fleetio. Retrieved October 22, 2021, from https://www.fleetio.com/blog/7-habits-of-highly-effective-fleet-managers

Cullen, David. (2018, April 5). *Should fleets own or lease trucks?* Trucking Info. Retrieved October 20, 2021, from https://www.truckinginfo.com/279778/should-fleets-own-or-lease-trucks

Corporate Fleet Services. (n.d.). *The different types of commercial vehicle leases.* Corporate fleet. Retrieved October 20, 2021, from https://www.corporate-fleet.com/the-different-types-of-commercial-vehicle-leases/

Cover Wallet. (n.d.). *Tips on how to hire truck drivers and when to invest in talent.* Retrieved October 22, 2021, from https://www.coverwallet.com/business-tips/how-to-hire-a-truck-driver

Commercial Capital LLC. (n.d.). *How to find trucking contracts.* Retrieved October 23, 2021, from https://www.comcapfactoring.com/blog/how-to-find-trucking-contracts/

Digital Edge. (2021). *Top 5 benefits of starting a trucking business when you are young.* Retrieved October 13, 2021, from https://digitaledge.org/top-5-benefits-of-starting-a-trucking- business-when-you-are-young/

Driver Knowledge Tests. (n.d.). *Types of trucks and trailers and what they carry.* Retrieved October 20, 2021, from https://www.driverknowledgetests.com/resources/types-of-trucks-and-trailers-and-what-they-carry/

eCapital. (n.d.). *How to get your trucking business invoices paid faster.* Retrieved November 4, 2021, from https://ecapital.com/en-ca/blog/freight-factoring/how-to-get-your-trucking-business-invoices-paid-faster/

eCapital. (n.d.). *How do trucking companies make good money?* Retrieved October 21, 2021, from https://ecapital.com/en-ca/blog/freight-factoring/how-do-trucking-companies-make-good-money/

Express Fright Finance. (2016, October 20) *How to build a diverse customer base for your trucking company.* Retrieved October 26, 2021, from https://expressfreightfinance.com/build-diverse-customer-base-trucking-company/

Engs. (n.d.). *Getting paid: 4 Effective collection strategies.* Retrieved November 5, 2021, from https://engsfinance.com/transportation/getting-paid-4-effective-collection-strategies/

Forbes. (2020, Feb 12). *13 Tips for building up your business' emergency fund.* Retrieved November 5, 2021, from https://www.forbes.com/sites/forbesfinancecouncil/2020/02/12/13-tips-for-building-up-your-business-emergency-fund/?sh=5b569f32120e

Faster Truck. (n.d.). *5 Benefits of starting your own trucking business.* Retrieved October 13, 2021, from https://fastertruck.com/pages/5-Benefits-Of-Starting-Your-Own-Trucking-Business.html

Forrest, Jason. (n.d.). *Buying a truck: Should you get a new or used rig?* Rigbooks. Retrieved October 20, 2021, from https://www.rigbooks.com/resources/buying-truck-should-you-get-new-or-used-rig

Fueloyal. (2017, November 2). *Your checklist for trucking permits and licenses.* Retrieved October 19, 2021, from https://www.fueloyal.com/your-checklist-for-trucking-permits-and-licenses/

REFERENCES

Fleet Owner. (2020, Feb 13). *Five modern methods for attracting, retaining truck drivers.* Retrieved October 22, 2021, from https://www.fleetowner.com/perspectives/ideaxchange/article/21122851/five-modern-methods-for-attracting-retaining-truck-drivers

For a Financial. (2018, September 7). *How to market your trucking business.* Retrieved October 23, 2021, from https://www.forafinancial.com/blog/industries-we-serve/market-trucking-business/

Girsch-Bock, Mary. (2020, December 20). *Why you need to create an emergency fund for your business.* The blueprint. Retrieved November 5, 2021, from https://www.fool.com/the-blueprint/business-emergency-fund/

Heathfield, M. Susan. (2021, February 20). *Top 10 tips for hiring the right employee—everytime.* The balance careers. Retrieved October 22, 2021, from https://www.thebalancecareers.com/top-tips-for-hiring-the-right-employee-1918964

Harrison, C. (2020). *Trucking Business Startup 2021–2022: Step-by-Step Guide to Start, Grow and Run your Own Trucking Company in as Little as 30 Days with the Most Up-to-Date Information (Starting Your Business).* Muze Publishing.

Hino. (2016, October 27). *5 Best ways to market your trucking business online.* Retrieved October 27, 2021, from https://

www.hino.com.au/blog/5-best-ways-to-market-your-trucking-business-online/

Johnson, Justin. (n.d.). *Safety in truck company operations.* Chron. Retrieved October 16, 2021, from https://smallbusiness.chron.com/safety-truck-company-operations-78202.html

Jones, Jenn. (2019, June 27th). *Types of vehicle leases.* Lending Tree. Retrieved October 20, 2021, from https://www.lendingtree.com/auto/types-of-vehicle-leases/

K & J Trucking. (2018). *Benefits of starting your own trucking business when you're young.* Retrieved October 14, 2021, from https://blog.drivekandj.com/benefits-of-starting-your-own-trucking-business-when-youre-young

Kahaner, Larry. (2019, Feb 25). *Tax law tips for trucking in 2019.* Fleet Owner. Retrieved October 19, 2021, from https://www.fleetowner.com/operations/finance-insurance/article/21703520/tax-law-tips-for-trucking-in-2019

Lahoti, Nitin. (2019, May 23). *How are technologies trans-forming the trucking industry.* Truck Pulse. Retrieved November 5, 2021, from https://mytruckpulse.com/blog/technology-innovation-in-trucking-industry.html

Lavinsky, Dave. (n.d). *Trucking business plan template.* Grow Think. Retrieved October 17, 2021, from https://www.

growthink.com/businessplan/help-center/trucking-business-plan

Lorenz, Gloria. (2014, January 26). *Choosing the best business structure for you*. Team Run Smart. Retrieved October 18, 2021, from https://www.teamrunsmart.com/articles/business-smart/business-management/january-2014/choosing-the-best-business-structure-for-you

Lemon Bin. (n.d.). *19 Different types of truck-do you know them all*. Retrieved October 20, 2021, from https://lemonbin.com/types-of-trucks/

Lowes. (n.d.). *Trailer buying guide*. Retrieved October 21, 2021, from https://www.lowes.com/n/buying-guide/trailer-buying-guide

March. (2017, Dec 20). *7 Truck technologies you need (and why)*. Fleet Owner. Retrieved November 5, 2021, from https://www.fleetowner.com/technology/article/21701619/7-truck-technologies-you-need-and-why

Motor Carrier HQ. (2020, Dec 15). *What to expect your first year as a new trucking company*. Retrieved October 15, 2021, from https://www.motorcarrierhq.com/2020/12/15/what-to-expect-your-first-year-as-a-new-trucking-company/

Motor Carrier HQ. (2019, July 17). *How to finance your startup trucking company*. Retrieved October 21, 2021, from https://www.motorcarrierhq.com/2019/07/17/how-to-finance-your-startup-trucking-company/

M., Keshavdas. (2021, January 7). *How to find trucking contracts*. Fleetrood. Retrieved October 22, 2021, from https://fleetroot.com/blog/top-11-ways-to-find-trucking-contracts/

MTA. (n.d.). *Membership benefits*. Retrieved October 30, 2021, from https://trucking.mb.ca/membership/membership-benefits/

Operfi. (n.d.). *Finding direct customers as a carrier*. Retrieved October 23, 2021, from https://operfi.com/finding-direct-customers-as-a-carrier/

OptimoRoute. (2021, October 22). *How to use fuel management systems to start cutting costs today*. Retrieved November 4, 2021, from https://optimoroute.com/fuel-management/

Overton, Travis. (2017, March 9). *Step 6: Different types of trucking companies*. CDL life. Retrieved October 15, 2021, from https://cdllife.com/2017/step-6-different-types-trucking-companies/

Patter, Jay. (2020, September 23). *10 Tips for better fleet management*. Real time networks. Retrieved October 22, 2021, from https://www.realtimenetworks.com/blog/10-tips-for-better-fleet-management

Pilon, Annie. (2016, Nov 22). *10 Reasons to choose leasing over owning a business vehicle*. Small business trends. Retrieved

REFERENCES

October 20, 2021, from https://smallbiztrends.com/2016/11/benefits-of-leasing-a-vehicle-for-your-small-business.html

PlanTemplate.com. (n.d.). *Trucking business plan template.* Retrieved October 17, 2021, from https://www.businessplantemplate.com/trucking-business-plan-template/2/

Pride Transport. (2019, October 09). *Is team driving right for you?* Retrieved October 22, 2021, from https://www.pridetransport.com/news-and-events/team-vs-solo-driving

Proline Trailers. (n.d.). *Things to know before purchasing a trailer.* Retrieved October 20, 2021, from https://www.prolinetrailersales.com/news/things-to-know-before-trailer-purchase

Proconnect. (2020, February 11). *How to calculate cost of freight shipping.* Retrieved October 30, 2021, from https://proconnectlogistics.com/blog/how-to-calculate-cost-of-freight-shipping/

Prime inc. (n.d.). *What are the benefits of team versus solo driving?* Retrieved October 22, 2021, from https://www.primeinc.com/trucking-blogs/what-are-the-benefits-of-team-vs-solo-driving/

Rasmussen, Roy. (2021, October 14). *Is the trucking business profitable? Challenges and opportunities.* Fastcapital360. Retrieved October 21, 2021, from https://www.fastcapital360.com/blog/is-the-trucking-business-profitable/

Rodela, Jimmy. (2018, October 23). *How much does it cost to start your trucking business?* KT. Retrieved October 22, 2021, from https://keeptruckin.com/blog/cost-starting-trucking-business

RTS. (n.d.). *How to write a business plan for your trucking company.* Retrieved October 17, 2021, from https://www.rtsinc.com/articles/how-write-business-plan-your-trucking-company

RTS. (n.d.). *License and permit checklist for starting a trucking company.* Retrieved October 18, 2021, from https://www.rtsinc.com/guides/license-and-permit-checklist-starting-trucking-company

Seppala, Erica. (2021, Feb 1). *Best business loans for owner operators, trucking companies, & transportation businesses.* Merchant maverick. Retrieved on October 21, 2021, from https://www.merchantmaverick.com/trucking-business-loans/

Shafer, Rebecca. (2011, April 24). *10 Safety program recommendations for trucking companies.* AMAXX. Retrieved October 16, 2021, from https://blog.reduceyourworkerscomp.com/2011/04/10-safety-program-recommendations-for-trucking-companies/

SST. (n.d.). *Technology that will revolutionize the trucking industry.* Retrieved November 6, 2021, from https://www.sttlogisticsgroup.com/blog/technology-that-will-revolutionize-the-trucking-industry

StealthPower. (2019, January 11). *8 Fuel management trends for fleet managers.* Retrieved November 4, 2021, from https://www.stealth-power.com/blog/8-fuel-management-trends-for-fleet-managers

Suburban Seating & Safety. (n.d.). *Solo vs. team truck driving: what you need to know.* Retrieved on October 22, 2021, from http://blog.suburbanseats.com/solo-vs-truck-driving-what-you-need-to-know/

Tafs. (n.d.). *How to write a trucking business plan.* Retrieved October 18, 2021, from https://www.tafs.com/business-plan-basics/

Tanke, Chris. (n.d.). *5 Mistakes to avoid when hiring truck drivers.* HNI. Retrieved on October 22, 2021, from https://www.hni.com/blog/bid/91389/5-mistakes-to-avoid-when-hiring-truck-drivers

Transport Topics. (2021, June 18). *Trucking turns from pandemic to prosperity.* Retrieved October 14, 2021, from https://www.ttnews.com/articles/trucking-enjoys-strong-freight-rebound-2021

Transport Service. (n.d.). *Five things to look for when purchasing a used semi-trailer.* Retrieved October 20, 2021, from https://blog.transportservices.com/five-things-to-look-for-when-purchasing-a-used-semi-trailer

Transmetrics. (2018, May 7). *Top 5 technologies and innovation trends revolutionizing trucking.* Retrieved November 6, 2021, from https://www.transmetrics.ai/blog/innovation-in-trucking/

TRUiC. (n.d.). *Business insurance for trucking companies.* Retrieved October 19, 2021, from https://howtostartanllc.com/business-insurance/business-insurance-for-trucking-companies

Truckx. (n.d.). *The technologies that can help trucking companies control insurance costs.* Retrieved November 6, 2021, from https://truckx.com/the-technologies-that-can-help-trucking-companies-control-insurance-costs/

Trucking Office. (n.d.). *Starting a trucking business: Invoicing and cash flow.* Retrieved November 4, 2021, from https://www.truckingoffice.com/blog/starting-a-trucking-business-invoices-cash-flow/

Top Mark Funding. (2019, December 4). *How much coverage do I need?* Retrieved October 20, 2021, from https://www.topmarkfunding.com/commercial-truck-insurance/

Top Mark Funding. (2019, December 31). *Trucking associations.* Retrieved October 29, 2021, from https://www.topmarkfunding.com/trucking-associations/

United States Department of Labor. (n.d.). *Trucking industry.* Retrieved October 16, 2021, from https://www.osha.gov/trucking-industry/safety-information

Vather, Elizabeth. (2018, May 15). *Fuel management tips for your fleet.* Samsara. Retrieved November 4, 2021, from https://www.samsara.com/blog/fuel-management-tips-for-your-fleet/

Vincent.M. John. (2019, January 31). *How does leasing a car work?* USnews. Retrieved October 20, 2021, from https://cars.usnews.com/cars-trucks/how-does-leasing-a-car-work

Wescott, Shelbi. (2019, Jun 28). *What is commercial truck insurance & how much will it cost you?* Merchant maverick. Retrieved October 18, 2021, from https://www.merchantmaverick.com/understanding-commercial-truck-insurance/

Made in the USA
Las Vegas, NV
05 November 2023

80294556R00100